THE CELTIC CHRISTIANITY OF CORNWALL

THE CELTIC CHRISTIANITY OF CORNWALL

DIVERS SKETCHES AND STUDIES

BY

THOMAS TAYLOR, M.A., F.S.A.

VICAR OF ST. JUST-IN-PENWITH

AUTHOR OF "THE LIFE OF DR. TAYLOR OF ASHBURNE"

First published in 1916.
Facsimile reprint by Llanerch Publishers,
Felinfach, 1995.

ISBN 1 897853 97 1.

Also published by Llanerch:

THE LIFE OF ST SAMSON OF DÔL
Thomas Taylor.

THE DROLLS, TRADITIONS & SUPERSTITIONS
OF OLD CORNWALL
Robert Hunt.

SCILLY AND ITS LEGENDS
H. J. Whitfeld.

NAENIA CORNUBIAE (The cromlechs & tumuli of Cornwall)
W. C. Borlase.

THE TRADITIONS AND HEARTHSIDE STORIES
OF WEST CORNWALL
W. Bottrell.

SYMBOLISM OF THE CELTIC CROSS
Derek Bryce.

THE CELTIC SOURCES OF
THE ARTHURIAN LEGEND
Jon Coe & Simon Young.

From booksellers. For a complete list, write to:
Llanerch Publishers, Felinfach, Lampeter,
Dyfed. SA48 8PJ.

THE CELTIC CHRISTIANITY OF CORNWALL

TO

M. JOSEPH LOTH

PROFESSEUR AU COLLÈGE DE FRANCE

IN GRATEFUL RECOGNITION OF A FRIENDSHIP
FROM WHICH I HAVE REAPED THE
FRUITS OF DISCIPLESHIP

Sed quanquam utilitates multae et magnae consecutae sunt, non sunt tamen ab earum spe causae diligendi profectae.

PREFACE

IN one of the most brilliant of modern books its author[1] calls attention to the common fallacy which assumes that "if you can find a principle which gives an adequate explanation of three different facts it is more likely to correspond with the truth than three different principles which give adequate explanations of the same facts severally."

This fallacy underlies much that is being urged in favour of a common origin for religious doctrines and methods of worship. A single source of religious belief or of religious phenomena is preferred to several sources as being more tidy and more in keeping with what we have learnt to expect in other departments of research. It may be illogical, but still it is recommended as a safe guide to the truth.

Indeed, it is difficult for a modern student to conceive how any real advance can be made in scientific pursuits unless the principle, which prefers one explanation of phenomena to many, is favoured.

Before the days of Kepler and of Newton it may have been possible, it may be possible still, to imagine more than one explanation of the fall of a heavy body to the ground and of the action of one inert mass upon another. The law of gravity, as elaborated by Newton, represents what, so far as we know, has

[1] R. A. Knox, *Some Loose Stones*. p. 89.

invariably happened and what we believe will invariably happen in space between two or more bodies, namely, that they will, as heretofore, each attract all the other bodies directly as their mass and inversely as the square of their distance. This law is not merely preferred before all other laws ; it is the very foundation of the whole of what is called Physical Astronomy. It is a law to which there are, within its own province, no known exceptions.

We accept this law not because we prefer one explanation to many, but because it meets not only the requirements of cases which might conceivably be explained in other ways but also the requirements of cases for which no other explanation has been suggested or conceived. Among laws, which are not received as self-evident, the law of gravity is unique. This will be clear to anyone who contrasts the secure position which it occupies with the perilous position occupied by laws which have been formulated within recent years.

Men do not prefer Newton's explanation to other explanations : the evidence in its favour is so overwhelming that they feel compelled to accept it.

It is far otherwise with other laws like evolution. These fascinate or repel from the very first. Preference undoubtedly enters into the complex intellectual process which leads us first to accept and then to defend this or that explanation of an array of facts. And this preference, admittedly illogical, may arise from our limited knowledge of the facts or from regard for some particular protagonist of one of many conflicting theories ; but, other things being equal, it seizes hold of that explanation which claims to cover the most ground and to reconcile the largest number of facts. It only becomes mischievous when it claims infallibility.

It is perhaps too readily assumed that in the domain of religious phenomena there is a law by which these phenomena are bounded and conditioned. Assuming such a law to exist, the attempts to formulate it will be directed in a greater or less degree by preference. For religious phenomena, by which is here meant the outward manifestations of religions, cannot be examined and classified, without a comprehensive knowledge of the religions themselves. And if, as a French writer has contended, "the man who would write the history of a religion must believe it no longer but must have believed it once," it follows that few persons, even in this versatile age, can claim to be proficient in more than three or four religions. From which it also follows that lack of knowledge must be supplied by fertility of imagination or by the exercise of preference on the part of him who employs the comparative method in order to discover the law.

And yet, it is only by eliminating this personal element and by confining our attention to material which is neither inaccurate nor defective that we can hope to arrive at the truth. It must be confessed that the rough and ready generalisations with which we are so familiar in this connection and the lack of care which is taken in gathering and sifting the materials upon which they are based, almost lead us to despair of useful results. The attempt to evolve a law from insufficient data is like an attempt to measure volume in terms of two dimensions or like an attempt to classify animals without an intimate knowledge of them. A salamander has four legs and a tail: so has a sheep. A zoology based on these criteria alone would not carry us very far. The biologist might kindly step in with his law of evolution and say some soothing words respecting their common origin, but we should leave off where we began and know no more of those animals than we did at the start, namely, that they each have four legs and a tail.[1]

In studying religions those points of resemblance which are most obvious are sometimes the most misleading. And for this reason. The essence of a religion —what may be called its soul—is not always revealed in its methods of worship. This is said to be especially true of Buddhism, at least by those writers who, like Mr. Feilding, strive to commend it to the Western world. Certainly it is no disparagement of a true religion that it should have, in the department of worship, many points in common with a false one. Every religion requires some machinery if it is to do its work. And it is more true to say of religions that they agree in machinery but differ in what they teach than to say that they agree in what they teach but differ in machinery. It would be most untrue, nevertheless, to assert that these common elements have always been acquired in the same way or have meant

[1] A friend of mine performed the surprising feat of evolving an entire system—god, religion, worshippers and all—out of much less than four legs and a tail. His only material consisted of a *word*, half-obsolete, of uncertain derivation and meaning. The jaw-bone in the hands of Samson was as nothing compared with the magic of this word in the mind of the valiant expositor of prehistoric religions. While reading the paper in which he proclaimed his discovery to a learned society, one could not fail to note the profound impression which it made upon the hearers or to admire the transparent sincerity of the reader.

It will not surprise those who read this book to learn that its author spent some portion of the wakeful night which followed the reading of the paper in the composition of a simple liturgy to crown his friend's achievement.

the same thing or have been used with the same object. Before any deductions whatever can be legitimately drawn the religious phenomena must be submitted to the most rigorous scrutiny. Dates, places, distances count for more, whether the phenomena be prehistoric or historic, than almost anything save accurate definition. This will be clear if we take an imaginary case. Let us consider the eagle as an object of worship. In the year 4000 A.D. a popular archæologist of liberal views notes the immense number of brass eagles which are unearthed from beneath the sites of ancient churches, and inasmuch as no mention is made in history and no rubric is to be found in any of the old service books of the function assigned to the image of the king of birds, he comes to the conclusion that the Christians of the Victorian era were, in spite of much quarrelling concerning the point of the compass towards which the priest should stand at the altar and the use of lights and incense, united at least on one point—the worship of the eagle. He reflects that reverence for the eagle was as dear to the hearts of Roman soldiers as it was abhorrent to the Jews. He recalls the incident at Cæsarea. He does not forget that long after the Roman Empire had ceased to be an important factor in European politics the Jews were regarded with unreasoning hatred. Putting two and two together he comes to the conclusion that Christians, in order to emphasise their contempt for Jewish susceptibilities, admitted into their religious system the cult of the eagle and that this cult attained its high-water mark in the nineteenth century. If it be objected that such a notion is altogether preposterous and absurd, that it is, in fact, an insult to average intelligence to attempt to influence human judgment by a fiction so transparent, it ought to be sufficient to recall the erudite expositions of rock basins, stone circles and dolmens which, elaborated by men of the highest eminence, were welcomed as brilliant discoveries by a generation by no means remote. It is a common enough practice, but it serves no useful purpose to hold up the wisdom of one age to the scorn of another. There are two cautions which are needed in all ages ; the first, that eminence in one department of human learning does not, of itself, constitute a qualification to pass authoritative judgments in other departments ; the second, that as all knowledge, when unhindered, is progressive the present generation may indeed hope to have got somewhat nearer the truth than its predecessors, but in virtue of the same principle it is still far from its final stage.

Archæology which at the beginning of the nineteenth century could hardly claim to be regarded as a science, had by the end of that century attained to the highest rank as a science. It has not outlived the record of past mistakes and some years may yet have to elapse before its achievements are fully recognised.

It is impossible to discuss the Christianity of Cornwall in its earlier stages without devoting some space to its Celtic inhabitants. This is all the more necessary because in the county there are many monuments, both pagan and Christian, and in some quarters there has been a disposition to confound them. Only by referring the pagan monuments to their true place in pre-history is it possible to avoid this confusion.

For such knowledge as he possesses of archæology the writer is largely indebted to M. Joseph Déchelette's

Manuel d'Archéologie. There is no work in English which, based on sound principles, attempts, as this does, to cover the whole ground. Like the *Principles of Geology* the *Manuel* stands alone.

When the losses in human life, due to the Great War, come to be reckoned up and those losses come to be analysed, there will be few names to take precedence of that of M. Déchelette. The *Revue Celtique*, after expressing its profound regret for his death, says that after honouring France by solid and learned works, notably by his *Manuel d'Archéologie*—a unique monument of erudition—at the age of fifty-three, though not compelled to serve in the army, he chose to take part in the campaign and to die like a hero. An order of the day of the French army supplies particulars of his death. He was a captain in the 29th Regiment of infantry and was shot down while leading his company. With his men he had won 800 metres of ground. As he lay dying he asked his colonel whether they had kept the conquered ground, and being answered in the affirmative, he replied that he was happy that his death was of service to France. The writer finely adds, *Belle vie, et fin plus belle encore.*

In a small book like the present, there will necessarily be many points which deserve some fuller explanation than was possible, while here and there some points will seem to be unduly magnified. The chapter on St. Michael's Mount might, at first sight, seem to add little to the main subject, but in this case it was not so much the hope of gain as the fear of loss which had to be considered. Should the reader meet with phrases and expressions which appear to him inconsistent with a serious treatment of the subject the writer can only crave his indulgence and assure him that they were not altogether unprovoked.

Chapter III was in substance contributed to the *Truro Diocesan Magazine*; Chapter IV was read at a conference of the Kirrier Rural Deanery; Chapters V and VI were printed concurrently in the *Revue Celtique* and the *Journal of the Royal Institution of Cornwall.* For permission to reprint them their author tenders his thanks to those journals.

Besides the *Manuel d'Archéologie* there are two other works to which he is much indebted, Dom Gougaud's *Chrétientés Celtiques* and Miss Clay's *Hermits and Anchorites of England.* No better introduction to Celtic Christianity could be desired than Dom Gougaud's book. Miss Clay has treated her subject with a particularity which is as rare as it is valuable, and although her book furnished little material for the present work, it was of great value in supplying the cartography of an unfamiliar region.

To Professor J. Loth and to Mr. H. Jenner, F.S.A., his obligations are of a more personal character and therefore more difficult to express. To both of them, in all matters which concern Celtic language and literature, he stands in the relation of pupil to master. As such he acknowledges gratefully their friendly and patient guidance and ever ready help.

It should be needless to add that in so doing he has no wish to shelter himself behind great names. For all blundering and backsliding he and he alone is responsible, inasmuch as throughout the perilous adventure he has cheerfully bestridden his own beast.

CONTENTS

APPENDICES

CORRIGENDA

p. xv, last line but one, for "Each" read "All."
p. 48, line 22, for "but which, as" read "when."
p. 48, line 24, omit "is."

THE CELTIC CHRISTIANITY OF CORNWALL

I

COINCIDENCE AND RESEMBLANCE

THE tyranny of observed coincidence and resemblance over the human mind is very remarkable, especially when coincidence and resemblance are associated with traditional sayings and superstitions.

Thirteen persons sit round a dinner table. When dinner is over the discovery is made that they were thirteen in number and the diners reflect that, according to the ancient fiction, one of them at least will die within the year. During the year one of them dies, as an insurance agent would have told them was extremely probable. A succession of such coincidences does not lead them to study the insurance tables, or to calculate the expectation of life; it only helps to confirm the superstition.

The sight of one magpie by the road-side alarms: the sight of two encourages. At the end of the day the single magpie is recalled when reckoning up the day's disappointments.

The devout Christian believer is not more prone to superstition than others. A man lay dying of consumption at St. Just. He was a crack rifle shot, an unbeliever and inclined to suicide. He insisted upon having his rifle by him as he lay in bed and, for the sake of peace, his wife allowed it. A single magpie came and perched daily on the hedge outside his bedroom window. One day seizing his weapon and steadying it on his knee as he lay there, he shot the magpie. The death of the solitary bird brought peace and all thought of suicide was banished and forgotten. The above are examples of superstition in the sense in which the word is here used.

But the shepherd's proverb :

> "A rainbow in the morning is the shepherd's warning :
> A rainbow at night is the shepherd's delight."

and the fisherman's

> "When the wind is in the south
> It blows your bait into the fish's mouth."

are based upon sound observation and contain no taint of superstition ; they could doubtless be referred to recognised scientific principles.

Again, the study of biology has led men to look, not in vain, for resemblances between the gills of a fish and the lungs of a mammal, between the hands of a man and the forefeet of a quadruped. Postulating the theory of evolution a common origin is discovered in either case.

The prehensile and tentacular movements of certain plants call to mind the like movements of certain fishes. Whether by means of the same theory, with the aid of the accredited results of research, they can be held to have had a common origin ; whether, for example, they can be referred to some such quality or instinct as that which characterises the *Proteus animalcule* is perhaps an open question. It seems, however, quite clear that these blind, involuntary movements on the part of fishes are not derived from the similar movements of plants or vice versâ, but that, if a common origin is to be found, it must be sought in some very early stage before animal and vegetable became differentiated. The evolution hypothesis, whether it be regarded as proved or unproved, is in any case invaluable because it stimulates thought, observation, and research. By means of it knowledge becomes coherent, articulate, scientific.

The application of this principle to religion is becoming more and more the vogue, and, provided that its adherents are content to work on the same lines as the students of physical science, there is no reason why useful results should not be obtained. There is, however, a tendency to transmute this working hypothesis into a superstition which, in point of sanity, is only comparable to that of the number thirteen and that of the single magpie—the superstition, in short, which notes coincidences and resemblances and ignores their opposites.

It is by no means clear that resemblance of rite and ceremonial and coincidence in point of time of calendared festivals furnish the proper material from which to formulate the law and to determine the source of religious observance. For example, however we may judge of the Salvation Army, it is obvious that a very different principle underlies and animates Mr. Booth's following from that which inspires the soldiers of King George. Military organisation merely suggested a useful and convenient form of discipline. In this case resemblance is utterly misleading, and the archæologist of the distant future, who should argue that the venerated coat of the General, supposing it to have been preserved, points to some mad but futile attempt to repeat the religious conquests of Mahomet, would be quite as wide of the truth as he who should seek the General's prototype in the militant ecclesiastic of the Middle Ages.

A further danger attends the student of religions. This arises from prepossession rather than from hypothesis and leads him to mistake deduction for induction. He finds, we will suppose, what he takes to be a latchkey. It is an instrument considerably the worse for wear and of a somewhat unusual pattern. He is quite certain it is a key. There is no room for doubt. He determines to find a lock which it will fit. Starting with the key he examines locks prehistoric, mediæval and modern, but all in vain, for the simple reason that the implement in his hands is not a key at all but the head of a fish spear.

It is not the critical method of induction but the uncritical method of deduction which is to be reprobated. When, for example, we discover by observation, the practical universality of sacrifice as a distinguishing mark of religion, we may explain the fact in a dozen different ways, but in every case we are compelled to recognise the belief in a God of some sort, and when we find that generally, at some stage of religious development, sacrifice is offered by way of propitiation, we are led to the conclusion that safety and salvation were held to be only possible by atonement. We have before us a multitude of locks and one key fits them all, and we are therefore led to conclude that *au fond* offence and sacrifice are related as poison to antidote. When, however, we descend to particulars, resemblances and coincidences are found to be as misleading as the salvationist's tunic. Their evidential value, to use a threadbare but useful phrase, is infinitesimally small and sometimes a negative quantity.

Relying upon resemblance, a person might be led to conclude that it was the spring turnip which suggested the shape of the watch and the duck's egg the morphology of toilet soaps.

Utility and convenience have entered largely into the ritual systems of all religions. The same accessories are required for the worship of Baal as for the worship of Jehovah. To identify Baal with Jehovah is to beg the question and to fall a victim to the tyranny of coincidence and resemblance.

When attempts are made to discover a common origin for the Christian Eucharist, the Aztec communion described by Prescott, and the ceremonial eating and drinking practised by the worshippers of Mithras, it is often assumed that the closer the ritual resemblance between them the stronger the argument in favour of a common origin. It does not seem to have occurred to the maintainers of this hypothesis that public worship, of whatsoever kind it may be, finds expression in a symbolism of its own, just as thought expresses itself in speech and in written language. The fact that Christianity expressed itself in symbol and sacrament does prove that from the very first it claimed to be a religion and not a mere philosophy or school of thought, but it does not prove identity of origin or of intention with the pagan religions which employed the same or similar symbolism. It was inevitable that the Christian Passover should have been singled out in order to illustrate the prepossession that in origin it is essentially pagan. In this case, however, it is not resemblance but coincidence (in point of time) which is supposed to afford the ground of proof. One writer, at least, who rightly connects it with the Jewish Passover, in order to exhibit its sacrificial character,[1] does not hesitate to refer its origin to the worship of Attis or Tammuz, the earth-god, on the ground that the time of its occurrence roughly coincides with the solemnities of Attis. No better illustration of the tyranny of observed coincidence could be found than in his ingenious but futile attempt to apply the principle to Cornwall. His object is to identify the May-day festivities, which he conceives to be a survival of Beltane solemnities, with those of the Christian Passover. Unfortunately for him the latter festival occurs too early; it can never occur later than the twenty-fifth of April. But he has read of Little Easter, which occurs a week later, and attributing to the Cornish a preference for a réchauffé of the Easter banquet to the banquet itself—a preference for which no reasons are vouchsafed—he concludes that Little Easter is the Cornish equivalent of the Beltane Feast. It might have occurred to the maintainer of this opinion to test it by means of the same calculations which forbade the synchronising of Easter itself with the pagan solemnity. Had he done so he would have found that Little Easter (Paskbian) or Low Sunday occurs in May only once in sixty or seventy years, and on May-day less than once in a century.[2] A coincidence which occurs once in a century does not convince the writer and will hardly

[1] R. A. Courtney, *The Hill and the Circle*, p. 15.

[2] Between the years 1854 and 1930, inclusive, Little Easter occurs once—on the 2nd of May, 1886.

convince the reader of the identity of the Celtic feast of Beltane with the Christian Passover, or even with the Low Sunday celebration at Lostwithiel described by Richard Carew, the historian.[1]

It is impossible, without destroying the character of this enquiry, to consider the Christian Passover in all its bearings upon the subject before us, but a few remarks are needed in order to place it in a right relation to the more ancient solemnity from which incidentally it sprang.

The Jewish Passover was kept at the time of the first full moon which followed the vernal equinox. The primitive Christians of Asia Minor, claiming for precedent the practice of St. John the Divine, commemorated our Saviour's Passion on the same day as the Passover and His Resurrection on the third day after. Thus it frequently happened that the very event which had led to the observance of the first day of the week as the Christian Sabbath had its yearly commemoration on some day which was not the Christian Sabbath. On the other hand, the Christians at Rome, following as they believed the practice of St. Paul, kept not only the weekly but also the yearly feast of the Resurrection on the first day of the week and the anniversary of the Passion on the third day before, in other words they kept their Paschal feast as we do now on the first day of the week which occurred next after the first full moon following the Spring equinox. The origin and signification of the feast were the same for both Eastern and Western Christians. It was the Christian Passover (*Pascha*) and was known by that name. The ancient Cornish word for it was Pask. In North

[1] Quoted in the *Parochial History of Cornwall*, iii., 175.

Staffordshire forty years ago it was the custom, and it is probably still the custom, for bands of men and maidens to solicit Pace (Pasch) eggs. The use of the term Easter, of Saxon origin, is merely a proof of the stubborn independence of the English character which refused to receive not only the names of the days of the week but also of the Christian seasons from the Latin. The coincidence in point of time of the Paschal feast with a pagan feast, if such coincidence can be discovered, was purely accidental; and the same can be said of Ascension, Pentecost and all other movable feasts which are ancillary to or supplementary of it. In this connection it is noteworthy that throughout the bitter controversy, dating from an amicable discussion held in the year 162 when Polycarp, bishop of Smyrna, paid a visit to Anicetus, bishop of Rome until the sixth century, it never occurred to either party to suggest a pagan origin for the feast or to connect the time of its celebration with nature or nature worship.[1] As the commemoration of a notable historical event—the Resurrection of Jesus Christ—it was observed by East and West, just as the Jewish Passover was observed as the anniversary of the "self-same day that the Lord did bring the children of Israel out of Egypt by their armies," and of that hurried meal of which a lamb of the first year and unleavened bread were the more important constituent elements. In the Bible and in the Primitive Church the two feasts are so closely linked together that, in order to demonstrate identity of origin for the Christian Passover and the feast of Tammuz the earth-god, it will be

[1] The Celtic controversy respecting the incidence of the Christian Passover was concerned solely with astronomical calculations and has, of course, no bearing upon the matter here under discussion.

necessary to show that the Jewish Passover derived its *raison d'être* from the same source as the worship of Tammuz. That any such source has been found or that any connection has been found, or will be found, is not to be taken for granted. The connection between the Jewish and the Christian Pascha is not open to dispute. Had the Christian Church repudiated the Pascha and kept a festival of the Resurrection entirely distinct from it, something might have been urged in favour of a pagan origin. It is the indissolubility of their union which forbids any such interpretation.

The writer has no desire to be regarded as an obscurantist and, for this reason if for no other, he offers to the students of folklore in general and to all deductive philosophers obsessed with the unique evidential value of coincidence and resemblance in particular, the following facts, for the authenticity of which he is prepared to vouch whenever he is required so to do. He believes that when their import is fully grasped they will carry, to the minds of the said philosophers to whom the discovery, never previously announced, is humbly but confidently dedicated, the conviction that not in Asia, the accredited home of mystery, not in Africa the cradle of theologies old and new, not in America the foster mother of science Christian and otherwise, but in Australia will be found the true origin of the Easter festival and its ceremonial. He regrets that his command of scientific language is unequal to the task which a discovery of such absorbing interest and far-reaching possibility demands. He therefore craves the indulgence of the learned for expressing himself in terms which he hopes will be intelligible to learned and unlearned alike.

In the low-lying land which borders Halifax Bay in the colony of Queensland there is to be found an edible root called the bulgaroo which, at the time of the European Spring equinox, after the heavy rains which begin in the month of February, betrays its presence by sending forth shoots of a bright and tender green colour. For some occult reason this root is preferred by the aboriginal inhabitants to the choicest delicacies which the white man, notwithstanding his cultivated taste in the matter of food and drink, can supply. Accordingly every year the black man, if employed, seeks his master's permission for a month's sojourn in the land of the bulgaroo. It is well known to all who have lived in Queensland that the black man is a keen observer of the heavenly bodies and is much distressed by the sight of an eclipse of the sun or moon, from which it may be inferred that he rejoices when the sun and moon are not obscured. Whether, strictly speaking, he can be described as a sun worshipper has not been determined, but it is believed that the disclosure of these particulars will help incidentally to solve this as well as the larger problem under discussion. The coincidence of the Spring equinox with the resurrection of the said bulgaroo from its dark retreat under the earth, and of both events with the assembling of the aboriginal tribes and of their partaking together of what may not unfitly be described as the root of ages (for in all probability we have here a vegetable food known to the black man's ancestors long before they emerged from a pre-human archetype); above all, the addition to the bulgaroo banquet of human flesh whenever it may be safely had, and the marked preference for those portions of the human body which, like the heart, are essential to life, and therefore, as they suppose, are the better fitted to stimulate and increase the eater's physical courage and efficiency; to which must also be added the attendant dance and song of corroboree and the more secret and mysterious bora meeting whereat, after due proof has been given, both oral and experimental of the candidate's fortitude, he is admitted to the full privileges of manhood by a solemn rite of initiation: all these ceremonial acts, whose significance it is impossible to misinterpret and to exaggerate, strengthened and not weakened (as might be supposed by a superficial observer) by the fact that at the antipodes Spring synchronises with European Autumn, establish a strong presumption that the continent of Australia affords the veritable solution of the great problem of the origin of Christian ceremonial observance. Nor is this surprising when we remember that according to an eminent German archæologist, Dr. Buttel-Reepen,[1] the Australian aborigines are the direct descendants of the propithecanthropi, i.e. pre-ape-men or common progenitors of apes and men, "since their foot had not yet undergone the definite change from a grasping organ to a supporting apparatus." Nay more, when we reflect that from the great concourse of pre-men one huge horde poured away in the direction of Africa, some of its members pursuing their wanderings through generations, until they eventually reached Europe across a bridge of land that then united the two continents; being accompanied in their migration by the pre-glacial fauna, the *Elephas antiquus*, *Rhinoceros merckii* and other great beasts whose fossilised remains bear witness of this emigration,

[1] Buttel-Reepen, *Man and His Forerunners*, pp. 72–3.

we are driven to conclude that throughout incalculable periods of time, from the Tertiary era at least, when, according to Dr. Woodward, man was already emerging from his pre-ape condition, down through the ages, palæolithic, neolithic, bronze, and iron, across continents which have been overwhelmed or refashioned, this simple meal of bulgaroo has persistently held its ground and won its triumphs in the social and afterwards in the religious life, pagan and Christian, of man as he has progressed steadily but surely from generation to generation.

Absurd as the foregoing presentment of a few, plain verifiable facts will appear to the reader, it is neither more absurd nor more wildly fantastic than much that passes for penetration with those who allow themselves to become the slaves of resemblance and coincidence. So far as the bulgaroo feast is concerned, it would be possible to write in the same grandiloquent manner and with an equal amount of wisdom of a beanfeast at Blackpool.

To resume. The deductive philosopher having identified the Christian Passover, which in England is commonly known as Easter and which always occurs in March or April, with the Celtic feast of Beltane which always occurs in May, it would be strange if he did not discover a pagan archetype for Christmas.

In this case both coincidence and resemblance point to the birthday of Mithras the Persian sun-god whose worship was introduced at Rome in the time of the Emperors. Is it unfair to remark that here conviction is rendered doubly certain by reason of the fact that the date of the earliest Christian observance of the Christmas festival is somewhat obscure? We know that it originated at a very early period and that the Alexandrians and the Churches of Palestine kept it, until the year 428, at Epiphany[1] and not on the 25th of December. Clement of Alexandria, who died about A.D. 220, refers to calculations of the year and day of the Lord's nativity not to encourage but to caution. It is noteworthy, however, that he gives no hint of the danger which might arise from the possibility of its being confounded with pagan celebrations of like nature. It is well known that a festival of the sun was held at the time of the winter solstice (*dies natalis invicti solis*), but it is equally well known that the early fathers never ceased to warn the people against confounding Christian festivals with pagan.[2]

Having satisfied himself that the keeping of Christmas originated in sun worship at the winter solstice, our philosopher would hardly do himself justice did he not discover a similar explanation of the commemoration of the birthday of St. John the Baptist at Midsummer. The ordinary uninstructed Christian would probably argue, and to better purpose, that if you keep the Saviour's birthday on the 25th of December you ought to keep the Baptist's birthday on the 24th of June, because the latter was six months older than the former.[3]

It is possible that pagan rites may have become associated with the Christian festival, but in Cornwall the Midsummer fires do not appear to have been so associated. Whatever their origin may be, there is

[1] The Armenians still keep the Nativity on the 6th of January.

[2] The subject is fully dealt with by Neander; *Church History* (Bohn's ed.), vol. ii., pp. 419–48.

[3] He would be led so to argue by reflecting that in the Church's Kalendar Ascension and Pentecost are similarly related to the Paschal Feast and Annunciation to Christmas.

no evidence that they have at any time entered into the Christian system.

The position for which, in the interests of truth, it seems vital to contend may be illustrated by citing a familiar episode from the life of St. Patrick—the episode of the Paschal fire. There is indisputable evidence that, from the days of the Emperor Constantine (A.D. 274–337) at least, Easter was distinguished by the Christian Church from other festivals by the lighting of fires or tapers to signify the rising of Christ from the dead to give light to the world. When St. Patrick arrived at the hill of Slane, in sight of Tara, on the eve of the Christian Passover, he set about preparing for that great solemnity. He lighted the sacred fire. But it so happened that the then pagan Irish were, at that moment, equally intent upon keeping a festival of their own, and that their festival also involved the observance of a similar ceremony. They, too, had a fire to light, and the act of lighting by anyone except King Leoghaire himself, or by one of his ministers at a signal given by him, was punishable with death. St. Patrick in ignorance of the prohibition lighted his fire first, and the fire was seen by the King and his subjects at Tara. He would doubtless have acted as he did had he known of the edict ; but it was, as events soon showed, this particular transgression, insignificant enough in itself, which at once brought about the collision between him and Leoghaire.

St. Patrick manifestly was not consciously observing a practice of pagan origin. Whatever thoughts, memories or associations his fire kindled within him they were definitely Christian. We are not told what meaning the King's fire had for *him*. The casual onlooker would probably have seen little to choose between the one fire and the other : he might conceivably have regarded them as expressive of one and the same intention. Had a modern philosopher been present he would almost inevitably have discerned a common origin and therefore a more or less near relationship. Yet both would have been wrong ; the first, because the motives and intentions of Patrick and Leoghaire were *not* the same ; the second, because until a common origin has been shown any inference derived from similarity of ceremonial is apt to be misleading however reasonable it may seem.

An inference is misleading when it carries with it consequences which are irrelevant to the main facts upon which it is founded.

You cannot say that because the Christians used fire in their worship at Easter and the pagans also used fire in their worship, therefore the Christians adopted the practice from the pagans ; still less can you say that Easter originated in a pagan festival. All you can say is that fire, as an accessory of worship, was used by both, just as prayer was also so used by both. The paraphernalia (using the term in a neutral sense) of two religions may be precisely alike, while the religions themselves may be as wide as the poles asunder. And the complaint one has to make against much that is brought forward as evidence of a common origin for customs, both religious and secular, is that it is not evidence at all, and that though it be repeated or multiplied a thousandfold, it follows the familiar rule of mathematics and amounts to nothing. Even when legitimate inferences have been drawn from groups of observed facts, it is by no means uncommon to find them so manipulated by writers as to convey wrong and erroneous impressions. Having regard to the laws of the physical growth and development of organic matter and to other considerations of a more technical character it may be considered a legitimate inference that men and apes are descended from a common ancestor, but it is a misrepresentation of the inference to say that it implies that men are descended from apes. For although it may be a source of comfort to all English-speaking people to believe that their ancestors "either came in with William the Conqueror or went out in the *Mayflower*," it is clearly impossible for them to believe that they can all trace their descent either from George the Third on the one hand, or from George Washington on the other. A genealogical enthusiast may perhaps be pardoned for seeking to embrace as many of the elect as possible in his family tree, because even in his moments of deepest depression he can point to Adam as the common ancestor. The student of religions in like manner may be pardoned for desiring to express in tabular form the successive stages through which doctrines and rites have passed; have been developed, arrested, modified, governed and conditioned. But neither the genealogist nor the religious philosopher can be pardoned for mistaking a collateral for a direct ancestor.

The Christian Church has, with generous and ready welcome, received into her bosom all that could produce credentials of kinship, holding nothing as common or unclean, however unworthy its associations and however perverted its use in the past. Painting, music, poetry, drama, philosophy, architecture, ritual, organisation, each has found a place and received a fresh consecration as the result of its admission to the embrace of the true mother of them all. Only one barrier has she interposed—the barrier of heresy. She has always insisted that the postulant's real intentions should be clearly known. By sacrament, creed, and confession she has exercised every precaution to secure peace within her sacred walls. She has sacrificed popularity, endured persecution, incurred hatred in order that all her children should share the same affections, should speak the same things and think the same thoughts. This has ever been and is still her great offence, her unpardonable sin, in the eyes of those outside her communion, viz. that she has been so uncompromisingly true to herself. For this reason it might have been thought superfluous, or at any rate a more or less academic matter, to discuss the origin of her symbolism and its affinities. The human mind, however, almost inevitably, refuses to admit the appropriateness of a newly imported symbol unless its past associations are free from suspicion. Not only so, the student of religions obsessed with the superlative value of resemblance and coincidence, is apt to suppose that if he can show that the paraphernalia of Christian worship approximately resembles that of some pagan religion he has proved identity of intention and belief.

By way of reply it would be possible to argue, with greater force and to better purpose, that historically it can be shown that Christian worship would be, at this time, fuller, richer, more ornate, more attractive and possibly not less true to its supreme purpose if larger use had been made of the common sources of religious ceremonial. The history of heresy is, however, a sufficient refutation of the main contention. An examination of some particular forms which the pagan theory has assumed in relation to Cornwall will be given later on.

II

THE CELTS

IT is almost, if not quite, impossible to acquire a right perspective of the position which the Celts occupy in British history without examining the incidence of that position and some of its relationships by the light of the results of modern archæological research.

In Cornwall, as elsewhere, the prehistoric races which inhabited the county before the Celts appeared have left abundant evidence of their presence. That evidence, however, will be hard to discover in the warp and bent of character and in the physical development which doubtless all Englishmen have in some measure inherited from them, and towards which these extremely remote ancestors have to some slight extent contributed. We shall probably never know enough about any of them so as to be in a position to say of any one living in the county as we might say, for example, of an Irishman "that splendid act of daring or that hairbrained escapade must be set down to his Irish breeding." Yet, inasmuch as no one supposes that an incoming race commonly extirpates the race it supplants there is always the suspicion that the new race may have yielded to the moral influence or to the religious atmosphere of the old. History supplies us with instances of this triumph of spiritual over physical force, Christianity itself being the most striking instance of all.

For this reason it is necessary to go back to those ages which have been distinguished as palæolithic, neolithic, and bronze, in other words to those periods during which unpolished stone, polished stone, and bronze implements were in use,[1] in order to discover, if possible, whether as the tide of industrial progress flowed in, there are indubitable signs of an unbroken tradition of religious thought and practice which became articulate in the historic narrative of Julius Cæsar.

Mr. Clement Reid, F.R.S., has thought that he detected traces of the palæolithic age in the raised beach at Prah Sands,[2] and there is, a priori, no reason to suppose that his discovery will not be confirmed by further investigation. Quite the contrary; it is not unlikely that some of the implements which have been found in the county and which are now commonly regarded as belonging to the later stone age will be found to belong to the earlier. This consideration, however, has only a very indirect bearing upon the present enquiry, for it has not yet been shown that the men of the earlier period had any religious belief at all.

On the other hand, there is a very strong presumption that the races of the later period had, towards the end of it, religious beliefs more or less definite. In this connection there is no need to call attention

[1] A still earlier age, the eolithic, which in Sussex has supplied my school contemporary, Dr. A. Smith Woodward of the British Museum, with what he believes to be a link between man and his pre-human ancestor is not represented in Cornwall.

[2] *Geology of the Land's End District*, pp. 79–80.

to the different kinds of stone implements which have been found in Cornwall and which have been identified with this—the neolithic—period. It will be useful, however, to consider, very briefly, the more striking of its monuments, found chiefly in the west and, by reason of their size, styled megalithic. They are distinguished as dolmens sometimes but incorrectly termed cromlechs, cists (stone chests), circles, menhirs or long stones, and alignments of which there are comparatively very few in the county. All belong to the same period; all appear to have been erected by the same race. They are all found in greater numbers and of larger dimensions in Brittany. The general opinion of competent archæologists is that, with the exception perhaps of the menhirs, they are all sepulchral in character and with the exception of some of the cists that they all belong to the neolithic or else to the earlier half of the Bronze Age. The dolmens, of which Chûn Quoit and Lanyon Quoit are good examples, differ only in size and detail from the cists which are abundant in Cornwall, and which have been proved to be depositories for the dead by their contents. The circles probably performed the very useful function of marking and protecting either single graves, as many of the smaller ones are still found to do, or a more or less large collection of graves like a modern churchyard wall. The fact that some of the circles no longer surround human interments, or that some cists are found without circles to protect them, presents no difficulty to those who accept this explanation, but who at the same time admit a variety of use in the disposal of the dead and who have abundant proof of a bygone vandalism which is not unknown in Cornwall to-day. Stonehenge is not only larger and more elaborate, but of later date than most of the larger circles, being the only one in England which is constructed of hewn stone, all the rest being built of undressed stone. Even of this, for which, on that account, there might have been presumed a quasi-religious origin, Sir Arthur Evans, one of the most eminent of living archæologists, can only assert that "it is one of the large series of primitive religious monuments that grew out of purely sepulchral architecture."

Of alignments it is hardly possible to say more than this, that they are usually associated with circles and may have served as avenues to them. The menhirs, sometimes isolated and independent of other ancient remains and sometimes as, for example, at St. Buryan and Drycarn, sufficiently near to circles to suggest association with them, are even less easy to explain. Some of them are of enormous dimensions, like the Men-er-Hroeck at Locmariaquer in Brittany; some are so small as to be liable to be mistaken for the rubbing stones of cattle. The former must have required vast numbers of men to erect, and it is their weight and size which has invested both the smaller and the greater with an interest and importance which would otherwise have been lacking. It is probable that some of them served as boundary stones, some as guide posts, and others as stones of memorial, like those reared by Jacob at Bethel, Joshua at Jordan, and Samuel at Ebenezer. The isolated menhirs of the largest size, i.e. the true menhirs or great undressed stones, reared by human instrumentality, wherever no traces of burial can be found either underneath or near them, undoubtedly suggest a religious purpose. While there is nothing to connect them with nature worship,[1] as commonly understood, or with solar worship, it is difficult to conceive how they came to be erected unless it was either to commemorate a departed chief[2] or to serve as symbols or objects of religion. Reverence paid to the dead, at certain stages of human development, may and probably does imply a belief in life after death. These monuments are of the late neolithic age.

The transition from it to the Bronze Age took place in Europe, according to the best authorities, about 1800 years before Christ. Bronze gave place to iron about 900 years later. The use of bronze in Cornwall, judging from the comparatively small number of bronze implements which have been discovered in the county, and from the fact that for its manufacture both of its constituent metals are abundant, would seem to have been of shorter duration here than elsewhere. Bronze celts have been found in Lelant, St. Just-in-Penwith, St. Hilary, St. Mawgan-in-meneage, Gwinear and in a few other places, but the net result is somewhat disappointing.

It is, however, during this period that in Gaul we

[1] "*Le pretendu caractère phallique de quelques-uns de ces monuments n'est q'une conjecture chimérique qui a permis à certains esprits imagintaifs de se donner carrière.*" Déchelette, *Manuel d'Archéologic*, I, 431, n. 2.

[2] W. C. Borlase, *Nœnia Cornubiœ*, p. 99 :

"Wishing to put beyond dispute the origin and purpose of some few at least of these monoliths, and to ascertain if any were indeed sepulchral, the author . . . examined the ground round some half-dozen of them."

At the foot of a menhir at Pridden, St. Buryan, he found "a deposit of splinters of human bone." At the foot of a menhir at Trelew, St. Buryan, he found "a deposit of splintered bones similar in quantity and appearance to that found at Pridden." A precisely similar discovery was made at Trenuggo, Sancreed. Another at Tregonebris.

meet with two races, the Ligurian and Iberian, occupying lands east and west of the Rhone respectively. These races must not be identified too closely with the countries whose names they bear.

They appear to have followed different occupations, the Ligurians devoting themselves to agriculture and the Iberians to the keeping of sheep and cattle.[1]

It is remarkable that little evidence should have been discovered respecting the character of the religion of either race. A bronze disc from Ireland and a horse mounted on (not harnessed to) a six-wheeled curricle to one of the axles of which is affixed a disc, from Denmark, have been supposed to be emblematic of the Bronze Age sun worship of those countries. Again, the swan-shaped prow of Scandinavian boats has been recognised as a solar emblem, but the freedom with which that ancient bird has been treated for decorative purposes, leaves one somewhat in doubt as to its religious signification. No evidence of the use of either symbol has apparently been found in Britain or in Armorica.

If the distinction between Ligurian and Iberian can be sustained is it not possible that the latter if not both emblems were confined to the Ligurians and were introduced by them along with their religious associations as traders engaged in the overland amber traffic between the Baltic and the Mediterranean?

The same dearth of evidence meets us when we come to consider the cult of the bull and the sacred horns and that of the axe. Had this cult been peculiar to a pastoral people like the Iberians an irreverent

[1] This is shown by the presence of bronze sickles in Ligurian graves and their absence in Iberian.

mind might have been pardoned for suggesting that they hit upon a very appropriate symbolism. Unfortunately the Bronze Age of Britain and Armorica, whether Iberian or otherwise, supplies us with very few if any illustrations of it. Two bronze bulls of small size found in Morbihan have been claimed to represent it in Armorica. The bronze bull found in the Vicarage garden at St. Just, undoubtedly fashioned for a religious purpose, seems to have an equal claim; but until more evidence is forthcoming it is allowable to doubt whether the Minoan beliefs, associated with the bronze period in the Ægean, ever gained a footing in Britain. M. Déchelette has with great pains striven to show that the mythology and the metal were closely related, perhaps contemporaneous and coextensive[1]—at least this seems to be the general drift of his exposition. While yielding to no one in gratitude for his great work—a challenge to English archæologists—it seems to the present writer that, in dealing with the religious symbolism of the Bronze Age, so far as North-Western Europe is concerned, he has done little more than to show that the double axe (*bipenne*) of the Ægean has its analogue, perhaps archetype, in the single axe with handle (*hache simple et emmanchée*) which is found inscribed on some of the Armorican dolmens of an earlier age. Nor is it self-evident that either the sacred horns or the axe is a solar emblem, though both appear to have been received into the Minoan system.

When we leave the Bronze Age and come to the Iron, we enter upon what has been termed protohistoric archæology. Within about 300 years of its

[1] *Archéologie: Age du Bronze*, chap. xiii.

commencement we find ourselves in the presence of a race which has survived and has in a measure retained its individuality up to the present time.

The Celts, it is true, were only one of several races which from the east and north pressed westward and southward over Europe for a period of over a thousand years ; but no invasion has ever been more complete or the effects of an invasion more profound and permanent. The Celts became identified with our island to a greater extent than either of their successors, the Saxons and Normans. The second body of them imparted to it its name. In the fifth century before Christ they had reached the Atlantic and had begun to invade Britain although the main body were near the Danube. In 387 B.C., they sacked Rome, and in the succeeding century a section of them crossed the Hellespont, overran Asia Minor and eventually settled in what became known as Galatia.

The point of greatest importance at the present stage of our enquiry is that of the Celtic religion between the close of the Bronze Age and Cæsar's invasion of Gaul and Britain. Was it one of the many forms of nature worship which found the central object of its adoration in the glorious orb who in the words of the Psalmist " cometh forth as a bridegroom out of his chamber and rejoiceth as a giant to run his course " ? Did the worship of the sun form its most prominent distinguishing feature ?

The much-quoted passage given by Diodorus the Sicilian, who lived in the first century before the Christian era and who reproduced it from the *Description of the World* written by Hecatæus in the fifth century, states that in the island of the Hyperboreans over against Celtica there is a magnificent circular temple which they have erected to Apollo.[1] The passage presents more than one difficulty. The Hyperboreans were known to the ancient world as the possessors of the sources of amber, a substance which is not found in Britain but in the neighbourhood of the Baltic. Those who would identify the Hyperborean island with Britain and the temple with Stonehenge, have to face the greater difficulty of accounting for the fact that a sepulchral structure erected in pre-Celtic times was, in the fifth century before Christ, being used for sun worship by Hyperboreans who may or may not have been Celts, but who in the passage are described as having erected it for that purpose. It should be remembered that Hecatæus had been dead for over a century when Pytheas the daring Greek explorer made his famous voyage of discovery, and that if that voyage was, as M. Déchelette contends,[2] to the navigator of the fourth century before the Christian era what a polar expedition is to the navigator of to-day, it is hardly likely that Hecatæus could have had very reliable information concerning either Britain or its Celtic inhabitants.

It may, perhaps, be allowable to hazard an opinion which after all is only an opinion, viz. that the Ligurians who dwelt along the transcontinental amber route were sun worshippers, but that until the days of Julius Cæsar we know very little, if indeed anything for certain, of the religion of the Celts who inhabited western Gaul and Britain. Whether Stonehenge was the temple referred to is very doubtful;

[1] Quoted by Déchelette, *Archéologie*, II, pp. 413, 567; by Lord Avebury, *Prehistoric Times*, p. 132; by D. Gougaud, *Chrétientés*, p. 13.

[2] *Archéologie*, II, p. 30.

whether it was orientated with respect to the sun is a matter which, as Professor Oman justly observes, need not be taken seriously.[1]

But what of the Phœnicians, and where do they come in? It is a cruel thing to say to a generation which can ill afford to part with any fragment of its diminished archæological patrimony, but it must be said without reserve or qualification: the Phœnicians do not come in at all.

It would be comparatively easy, as some have already found, to provide Celtic Britain with all the elaborate machinery of sun worship if it could be shown that there were direct and close relations between Britain and Phœnicia either before or after the Celtic invasion. No one, of course, doubts or denies the glory of the Phœnician thalassocracy. The Bible is only one of many witnesses. Hiram King of Tyre supplied Solomon both with craftsmen for the brass work of the Temple at Jerusalem and with sailors for his trading expeditions to India. Gades (Cadiz) the port of Tartessus, or Tarshish, was founded by the Phœnicians before 1100 B.C. The ships of Tarshish are rooted in the memory like the bulls of Bashan and the cedars of Libanus. Ezekiel's lamentation for Tyre[2] is not only one of the most profoundly pathetic but also one of the most illuminating passages in the Old Testament.

Speaking of Tyre, he says, "Tarshish was thy merchant by reason of the multitude of all kind of riches, with silver, iron, tin, and lead they traded in thy fairs:" "the ships of Tarshish did sing of thee in thy market: and thou wast replenished

[1] *England before the Norman Conquest*, p. 9.

[2] Ezekiel, xxvii and xxviii.

and made very glorious in the midst of the seas."

Nevertheless, great, extensive and varied as was the commercial enterprise of the Phœnicians, scholars are now generally agreed that they never got beyond Gades in their Atlantic voyages.

Moreover, the Cassiterides or Tin Islands, mentioned by Diodorus, which a former generation strove to identify with the Scilly Isles, lay undoubtedly to the north of Spain.[1] At the same time it must be noted that the same author Diodorus, who probably had his information from Poseidonius (born circa 135 B.C.), does expressly state in the same passage that tin was conveyed from Britain to Gaul and overland to Marseilles. By that time, however, the doom of Carthage, the daughter city of Tyre, situated on the Bay of Tunis, had also been sealed.

This absence of historical evidence respecting Phœnician intercourse with Britain, supposing such intercourse to have existed, might have been in some measure explained—and not as the Privy Council explained the Ornaments Rubric of the Church of England, by arguing that omission implies prohibition—by assuming that the source of the tin supply was kept secret, like that of amber, by the traders in that commodity. It is the fact that no vestige of these Semitic navigators has been found either in Gaul or in Britain, which decisively excludes the supposition that they ever visited those countries. Dr. Birch in giving his judgment upon the bronze bull found in the garden of St. Just Vicarage states it as his conviction that no object has yet been found in Britain which can be satisfactorily identified with

[1] Sir Hercules Read, *Early Iron Age*, p. 85.

the Phœnicians,[1] and M. Déchelette is equally emphatic respecting the absence of similar objects in Gaul.[2] What M. Alexandre Bertrand says of Celtic civilisation, namely, that neither the Ligurians, nor the Phœnicians, nor the Greeks, nor the Iberians collaborated in that educational work, may with some reservations in favour of the two latter nations be accepted as true of the Celtic religion.

From Julius Cæsar some useful information is to be gained respecting the religion of the Celts of his own day. He states that they had many gods, the chief of whom, in Gaul at least, answered to the Roman Mercury, patron of arts and crafts. Mars, Apollo, Minerva and Dis Pater were represented in the Celtic system, but it is not easy to equate them satisfactorily. After the Roman conquest the Britons followed the custom of other subject races and identified their gods with those of Olympus. Some of their gods found no corresponding analogue, like Nodens, whose temple overlooked the Severn ; others again were purely local and patronal.

During the three centuries while Britain remained a province of the Empire the Romanisation of the native religion had free scope, the spread of Christianity meanwhile striving with indifferent success to keep pace with it. "The larger half of the altars and shrines, discovered in Britain are simply set up to honour the ordinary gods of the Roman world."[3] Among these latter were many strange divinities, who in origin were neither Celtic nor Roman, but were those of alien races led to Britain by the hope of profitable traffic or by compulsory military service.

[1] *Arch. Journal*, viii, 8. [2] *Age du Bronze*, p. 29.

[3] Oman, *England before the Norman Conquest*, p. 107.

Mithras, for example, whose worship was introduced at Rome under the Emperors, found in this way a place in the British pantheon.

There is no evidence to show that either nature worship or sun worship was the dominant religion of the Celts either before, during or after the Roman occupation. It is, of course, possible to say of the Romans that they practised both, but it is an abuse of language to say that they were either sun worshippers like the Egyptians or nature worshippers like the Phœnicians. The same holds good of the Celts.

Under Roman influence the days of the week received Latin names derived from the planetary system, all of which except Sunday (*Dies Solis* which became *Dies Dominica*) continued to be used by our lawyers until English took the place of Latin in the courts of record. In Cornwall, notwithstanding the Saxon invasion, the Latin names were retained until Cornish ceased to be a spoken and written language. Thus Sunday, *Dies Solis* became *Dê Zil*, *Zil* being the Cornish derivative of Sol and not a variant of the Cornish word Houl.[1] Until the Roman occupation the Celts reckoned time by nights, not days. Thus the first night (of the week if they had weeks) was the sixth night after new moon, that is when the moon was on the point of becoming half-full. Their year, therefore, consisted of thirteen months. The Celtic mind appears to have revelled in the realm

[1] Mr. Henry Jenner, F.S.A., to whom I am indebted for this statement, has reminded me that St. Michael's Mount is given in the *Life of St. Cadoc* as Dinsul (Mons solis) and that Tregaseal in St. Just may be a compound of which *seal*=*Zil*=*sol*. Both are possible. Roman intercourse with the extreme west of Cornwall is proved by the Roman milestone at St. Hilary, which is within easy distance of both places.

of mystery. The practice of magic; the prevalence of human sacrifice; the numerous local divinities, with strange names preserved to us only in the dedications of their shrines, whose attributes and powers remain unknown; the hidden virtues of the mistletoe and the selago; above all, the secrets of the Celtic priesthood—the Druids—suggest, but unfortunately only suggest, a religious differentiation which carries us back to a period more remote than that of any religious system with which we are familiar.

Professor Sir John Rhys has attempted to show that Druidism was a pre-Celtic survival, the religious system, in short, of some race which preceded the Celts in Britain, and his judgment would doubtless have been accepted had there not been good evidence to show that the system was not peculiar to Britain but to the Celts themselves. It prevailed among the continental Celts just as it prevailed among those of Britain and Ireland. On the other hand, its affinities with classical mythology are not sufficiently pronounced at the time when it is first encountered to indicate an Ægean origin. When the original home of the Celt has been determined it may be possible to discover the home of his religion.

The Druids[1] were the interpreters of divine things to the Celtic conscience. They shared with the knights the administration of public affairs, expounded the ceremonial law and determined the times and modes of its application. Cæsar states, but not on

[1] Gougaud, *Chrétientés*, p. 22. The derivation of the word Druid is uncertain. There appears to be no doubt that the Druids practised a form of divination founded not on the flight but on the song of birds, that of the wren in particular. Dren is Irish for wren. From this some have inferred that Druid is derived from dren drui-én. There is another Irish word *drúi* (genitive *druad*) which meant a magician. Anwyl, *Celtic Religion*, p. 55.

good authority, that Druidism originated in Britain, and Tacitus, who lived towards the end of the first century of the Christian era, that Anglesey was its religious centre. An impressive picture is given of the scene (A.D. 60) which was presented to the army of Suetonius Paulinus preparing to attack that venerable sanctuary. "Along the shore was seen a dense line of armed warriors, while women were rushing about between the ranks garbed like the Furies, in black gowns, their hair flowing loose, and torches in their hands. The Druids were visible in the rear offering sacrifices to their gods, raising their hands to heaven, and calling down dire imprecations upon the head of the invader."[1]

Of Druidical worship in Cornwall there is no direct evidence.[2] The kinship and intercourse and close relations, however, which subsisted between Cornwall, Wales and Ireland leave no room for doubt that Druidism was its religious system. It should be needless to observe that its megalithic remains, dolmens, circles, and the like, which were erected many centuries before the Celts appeared in Britain, had originally no connection with Druidism and that there is no evidence to show that they ever became identified with it.

Without stopping to compare Irish and Gaulish Druidism with that of Britain there is one point which claims attention and which, whether Druidical or essentially primitive and sporadic, bears witness to the existence of a cult which, occurring in Ireland, could not have been introduced by the Romans.

[1] Prof. Oman's translation, *England before the Norman Conquest*, p. 74.

[2] See, however, chap. iv.

From the life of St. Patrick we learn that in Ireland idols of stone, sometimes adorned with gold, silver, or copper, and in particular one stone, that of Ceen Cruaich or Cronn Cruach, were worshipped by all the people of the land.[1] Practices similar though not necessarily identical—in other words idol worship—characterised the Cornish paganism of the sixth century. Henoc the biographer of St. Sampson relates an incident of such absorbing interest that a translation of the Latin,[2] however imperfect, will be welcomed. It was during the saint's sojourn at Docco (St. Kew) that we read, " Now it came to pass, on a certain day as he journeyed through a certain district which they call Tricurius (the hundred of Trigg) he heard on his left hand (*in sinistra parte de eo*) to be exact, men worshipping (at) a certain shrine after the custom of the Bacchantes by means of a play in honour of an image. Thereupon he beckoned to his brothers that they should stand still and be silent while he himself, quietly descending from his chariot to the ground and standing upon his feet and observing those who worshipped the idol, saw in front of them, resting on the summit of a certain hill an abominable image. On this hill I myself have been and have adored and with my hand have traced the sign of the cross which Saint Sampson, with his own hand, carved by means of an iron instrument on a standing stone. When Saint Sampson saw it (the image), selecting two only of the brothers to be with him, he hastened quickly towards them, their chief Guedianus standing at their head, and gently ad-

[1] D. Gougaud, *Chrétientés*, pp. 16, 17.

[2] Edited by M. Fawtier (Paris, Champion, 5 Quai Malequais, 1912). The Latin text is given in the appendix to this book p. 169.

monished them that they ought not to forsake the one God who created all things and worship an idol. And when they pleaded as excuse that it was not wrong to keep the festival of their progenitors in a play, some being furious, some mocking but some of saner mind strongly urging him to go away, straightway the power of God was made clearly manifest. For a certain boy driving horses at full speed fell from a swift horse to the ground and twisting his head under him as he fell headlong, remained, just as he was flung, little else than a lifeless corpse.

"Then St. Sampson, speaking to the tribesmen as they wept around the body, said, 'You see that your image is not able to give aid to the dead man. But if you will promise that you will utterly destroy this idol and no longer adore it I, with God's assistance, will bring the dead man to life.' And they consenting, he commanded them to withdraw a little further off and after praying earnestly over the lifeless man for two hours he delivered him, who had been dead, alive and sound before them all.

"Seeing this they all with one accord, along with the aforementioned chief, prostrated themselves at St. Sampson's feet and utterly destroyed the idol."

It will have been noticed that the writer does not state whether the idol was of stone or of wood; nor is it quite clear whether it was itself the object of worship or the representation or symbol of a god. Probably it was the latter.

Whatever its nature and character the saint decided upon its destruction and marked the sign of the cross not upon it but upon a stone standing in its vicinity. It does not seem likely that the word abominable (*simulacrum abominabile*) would have been employed to describe a wheel-headed stone. The idol was probably a fetich pure and simple or possibly a symbol of nature worship.

Whatever may have been the purposes for which menhirs were erected during the neolithic period and whatever adoration may have been paid them by succeeding races—we have no evidence that such adoration *was* paid—it appears certain that they had nothing to do with sun worship. The Minoan symbolism, as such, which included the cross or rather the wheel with four spokes (in this connection a better and more accurate description because it explains the most beautiful form which it assumed as the swastika), is entirely absent from the prehistoric monuments of Western Europe.[1] The stone crosses of Cornwall are not of an earlier date than the sixth or seventh century of our era, and by that time not only was the county actively Christian but the Minoan symbolism was dead, buried and forgotten.

Stones may be, and in many ages and in many lands have been, venerated for their supposed powers and virtues. Such stones, especially in Brittany, have received Christianisation, that is, have been marked with or surmounted by a cross within comparatively modern times. There is no reason why some such course may not have suggested itself to the Cornish Christians of the seventh and succeeding centuries. But the golden age of Celtic Christianity was during the latter half of the seventh and first half of the eighth century, and at that time Cornwall was in constant communication with Ireland, the centre of Christian learning.[2]

[1] Déchelette, *Archéologie Préhistorique*, p. 441.

[2] Oman, *England before the Norman Conquest*, p. 30.

About 270 stone crosses are to be found in Cornwall. They are mostly of granite and have been fashioned by means of iron implements, in some instances with considerable taste and skill.

They are too well known to require description. To suppose them to have been erected by sun worshippers in the sixth and succeeding centuries is to suppose the prevalence of a religion in Cornwall which at that time prevailed nowhere else in Europe and concerning which history is silent. On the other hand, to suppose them to have been originally connected with nature worship of a peculiarly revolting character and to have been Christianised by signing them with the sign of the cross is highly improbable if, as the maintainers of this hypothesis assert, that sign was regarded as pagan.

A much simpler and more convincing explanation is that the stone crosses were erected in order to disaffect and sanctify places which from time immemorial had been devoted to old pagan superstitions.[1] This at any rate has the merit of being in accordance with the facts disclosed by the Sampson episode. Moreover, it avoids the anachronism which connects them with sun worship, while at the same time it disallows the charge of incredible folly which must otherwise be imputed to the founders of Cornish Christianity if we suppose those earnest men to have retained a degrading symbol of nature worship with little or no modification of its structural features.

[1] Anatole le Braz, *La nuit des feux.*

III

CORNWALL AND BRITTANY

ALTHOUGH much good work has been done and useful results have been obtained in many fields of research both by individual Cornishmen and by societies like the Royal Institution of Cornwall, there is one department at least which has been somewhat neglected by those for whom it might have been expected to possess a special attractiveness.

The interest which of late years has been awakened in the Cornish language and in Celtic Christianity has not been the result of any revival in Cornwall itself. Mr. Whitley Stokes is an Irishman by birth and extraction, Professor Loth a Breton, Mr. Henry Jenner a Cornishman. In fact no Cornishman except the last-named has so far thrown himself wholeheartedly into the movement which has for its object the critical study of the language and religion of the Celtic-speaking nations. This is much to be regretted, because both of these subjects were assigned a place in the comprehensive scheme of Dr. Borlase, which, as conceived and elaborated by him, entitled him to rank among the leading European antiquaries of his own day. Although Dr. Borlase achieved little of permanent value in the way of exposition, he gathered much valuable material which, but for him, would have been lost, and by his sagacity and diligence succeeded in riveting the attention of his compatriots.

He was, like all the leading archæologists of his time, a resolute believer in the Druidical origin of the prehistoric remains of the county, a theory which he advocated with consummate skill and particularity. Since his death the theory has been found to be untenable without any serious injury, however, being done to his high reputation.

The brilliant essay of his great-great-grandson, the late Mr. William Copeland Borlase, on the *Age of the Saints*, first printed in 1878, has been one of the very few original works accomplished in the county having for its object the exposition of Celtic Christianity. In this work its writer attempted too much. Subsequent research has shown that many of his identifications of the Cornish saints are untrustworthy, and that his arbitrary delineation of the spheres of influence of the respective groups of Irish, Welsh and Breton saints is often fanciful and misleading.

Given leisure and the spirit of enquiry, the two subjects which ought to appeal most strongly to a Cornishman are the ancient religion and the ancient language of the county to which he belongs.

Both subjects are now well within his reach owing to the immense amount of material which has, within recent years, been made available by the publication of ancient records. The *Councils and Ecclesiastical Documents* of Haddan and Stubbs, the *Episcopal Registers*, edited by Hingeston-Randolph, the *Parish Registers*, edited by Phillimore and others, the publications of the Record Commissioners and of the Royal Institution of Cornwall, the *Revue Celtique*, the *Ancient Cornish Drama*, edited by Mr. Edwin Norris, the critical works of Mr. Whitley Stokes, of Professor Loth and Dom Gougaud, the *Cornish Grammar* of Mr. Jenner; these are a few of the many sources whence valuable information may be derived for the comparative study of these subjects. In this connection it may be observed that little satisfaction will be gained from facts and statements which are obtained at second hand. Facts must be sought out in the original documents and examined in their original settings.

The context is often more illuminating than the fact which it enshrines. Not documents only; the towns, villages, hamlets and homesteads, with their ancient names, address silent appeals to the hearts and understandings of those who live among them.

An interesting illustration is supplied by the three Cornish words, Eglos (*Ecclesia*), Escop (*Episcopus*) and Pleu (*Plebs*)—interesting because the final judgment must be held in suspense until a survey has been made of their ramifications. All three words are found in the place-names of this county. Eglos is found in Lanteglos, Egloskerry and in some other places; Escop is found in Trescobeas in Budock, formerly appendant to the bishop's manor of Penryn, also in Mainen Escop (Bishop's Rock), in the Isles of Scilly; Pleu is found in Plunent, the ancient name of Pelynt, in Pluvathack (Budock) and possibly in Bleu Bridge in Gulval. Names beginning or ending in Eglos are numerous in Cornwall; those having Pleu for the first syllable are very few in number. In Brittany very few place-names are composed of Eglos and Escop, whereas Pleu enters into many. Why does Pleu rather than Eglos lend itself so readily in Brittany to the exigencies of ecclesiastical nomenclature? Were it not that Lan (monastery) is equally distributed in the two countries, we should be tempted to say that in Cornwall a Celtic word (lan) was preferred to a Latin word (plebs) to describe the ecclesiastical unit. Some difference of condition or of association there must have been to account for it. That which most readily occurs is that Armorica was thoroughly Latinised before the insular Celts arrived there, whereas Cornwall was probably never brought into close contact with Roman civilisation as such except on and near the coast; in other words, that Plebs was in use in the former country before it became Christian and acquired afterwards a specific ecclesiastical signification, whereas in Cornwall it was introduced along with Christianity or after Christianity had taken root. Very few traces of Roman civilisation are to be found in this county. The Roman milestone at St. Hilary is almost unique. Roman coins, of which many have been found in the county, do not prove Roman settlement. It is certain, however, that Britain had become Christian, at least in name, before the Roman legions were withdrawn, and it is therefore probable that the words Eglos, Escop and Pleu had been received into the Cornish language before that time. And the true explanation of the persistence of Pleu in the place-names of Brittany seems to be that the insular Britons, who had acquired the word Plebs during the Roman occupation, converted it, for ecclesiastical purposes, into Pleu and took it with them when they emigrated to Armorica, where very soon it had to give place to the word Pares (from the French Paroisse), though not before it had taken root in the place-names. In Cornwall and Wales, on the other hand, Pleu remained in current use and is therefore seldom found in the place-names of those countries. Making allowance for changed conditions, the same explanation accounts for the persistence of the word Lan in the place-names of all three countries—it persisted in the place-names because it had fallen out of current use.

For reasons which will appear later, it is important to keep well in mind the relations which subsisted between Cornwall and Brittany from the time of the Dumnonian exodus, which began in the first half of the fifth century, until those relations were interrupted in the sixteenth century.

Leaving for future discussion the question of religion, there are points of contact between the two countries which deserve attention, not only because they are interesting in themselves, but because they can hardly fail to suggest others.

The colonisation of Armorica by the people of Dumnonia is accepted by every scholar of repute. The gradual re-settlement of Bretons in Cornwall is not so well known. Nevertheless, the historical evidence is not open to question. Domesday Book shows that, with three exceptions, all the landholders in Cornwall were, in the days of Edward the Confessor, Saxons. When William the Norman set about the conquest of England, he was joined by several Breton nobles, who, by way of reward, received considerable grants of land in Cornwall. Richard Fitz Turold, the ancestor of the baronial house of Cardinan, received thirty-one manors, Brient six, Blohiu five, Jovin thirteen, Wihumar three and Judhel one.

It was, doubtless, owing to the presence of these Breton knights that Cornwall came to play so important a part in the Arthurian romances, which, soon after the Conquest, became known throughout western Europe. There has been much controversy respecting their origin. They have been attributed to England, Wales, Cornwall and Brittany. That of *Tristan and Iseult* was, until quite recently, commonly referred to an English archetype which assumed literary form at the hands of British and Welsh minstrels or jugglers.

It has remained for Professor Loth to demonstrate, beyond the possibility of doubt, that it originated in Cornwall at a time when Celtic, Saxon and Norman were all spoken languages. Those who are familiar with the romance will have been puzzled by the presence of two Iseults in one and the same story. On this point M. Loth says, "in my opinion it is from the juxtaposition in Cornwall of two legends, the Cornish and the Armorican, and from a compromise between the two that the creation of the two Iseults has originated."[1]

No better proof could be found of the friendly spirit which existed between the two nations than their mutual consent to share the tales and traditions of both.

It was a Breton who, in 1177, carried away the body of St. Petrock to the monastery of St. Mewan in Brittany. As a canon of Bodmin he had learnt to venerate the saint, and doubtless considered that he could confer no greater boon upon his own countrymen than to present them with the saint's relics. At the instance of Henry II, Roland de Dinan restored them to the Priory.

[1] *Romans de la Table Ronde*, p. 110.

The trade between the two countries was considerable. The Patent Rolls supply ample evidence of this. In 1343 we find an inquisition respecting certain mariners of the county of Cornwall who had been received into the service of the Duchess of Brittany, but who had turned pirates and plundered the vessels of both countries.

More convincing still is the evidence supplied by the first subsidy roll of King Henry VIII. The roll is undated, but the date cannot be later than 1523. In it are given the names of all those who were required to contribute to the subsidy and the several amounts of their assessment, in land and goods, for the purpose. The roll for the hundred of Penwith is almost complete, only the parishes of Crowan, Illogan, Redruth and a part of Camborne being missing.[1] In all the Penwith parishes, save five of the smaller ones, are found Bretons who are described as *nati in partibus Britanniæ sub obediencia Regis Francorum.* These Bretons constitute more than one-sixth of the total tax-paying population of the hundred of Penwith. They are described as tinners, fishermen, smiths, servants, labourers and cooks : the occupations of twenty-nine of them are not given. Although the several amounts to be contributed by them are in every case in respect of goods and comparatively small, there is fortunately reliable evidence to prove they were not mere sojourners but persons who had come to stay.

The order to keep parish registers issued by Thomas

[1] The Roll was printed by the Royal Institution of Cornwall in 1887. Extracts from some of the later rolls are given by Mr. J. H. Matthews in his *History of St. Ives, Lelant, Towednack and Zennor,* pp. 133-42 ; and by Dr. W. J. Stephens in his *Collections for a History of Crantock.*

Cromwell in 1537, and the further order, in 1597, requiring a transcript of them to be made on parchment, would have provided future generations with an invaluable source of information, had those orders been generally obeyed and the records carefully preserved.

Unfortunately, few parishes can claim to possess an uninterrupted record of baptisms, marriages and burials from the year 1538 up to the present time. In Penwith only Camborne enjoys this distinction. All the rest of the registers begin after the accession of Queen Elizabeth. The earliest of the Madron registers, which begins in 1577, has been printed and is accessible: the Camborne marriages have also been printed. From these two registers it will suffice to give extracts which bear upon Breton settlement in the county. Camborne supplies the following marriages:

1538. John Carthowe, brito, and Nora his wife.
1540. Stephen Bryton and Jane his wife.
1540. G'ua Bryton and Margaret his wife.
1540. Uden John, brytton, and his wife.
1540. Gregorie Brytton and Margaret his wife.
1546. John Gerecrist and Margaret Willm, bryttons.
1568. Peres Brytton and Alson his wife.

If the above list is compared with the subsidy roll, to which reference has been made, it will be clear that Bryton is not a surname but a descriptive epithet. The list, in fact, supplies only four surnames, Carthowe, John, Willm and Gerecrist. Of these the first and last are interesting: the first survives in Cornwall as Carthewe and in Brittany as Carzou;

the last is a Breton place-name—Kergrist, near Pontivy.[1]

As showing that the Breton immigrants did not return to their own country the following entries from the Madron register[2] will be helpful, if not conclusive. Among the burials we have :

1582. Jane, wife of John Brittayne.
1585. Elizabeth, wife of Oliver, the Brittonn.
1587. Joane, wife of John Britton.
1599. Peres Brittayne.

Unfortunately the Madron baptisms are missing until 1592 and the marriages until 1577. It is impossible, however, with the Camborne marriages and the Madron burials before us, to resist the conclusion that in the first half of the sixteenth century Bretons arrived, married and were buried in the county. They doubtless left descendants. It is remarkable, however, that whereas, at the present time, in Cornwall the surname Britton or Bridden is rare, in the Midlands, where Breton influence was never considerable, it is comparatively common. The explanation appears to be that the Christian names of the Breton immigrants became surnames, and in this way the number of Christian surnames, which in West Cornwall now amounts to little short of 30 per cent of the whole number, was vastly increased.

For how long the tide of Breton immigration had

[1] I am indebted to Professor Loth for the identification of these surnames.

[2] Some further light would doubtless be thrown on the subject if the Camborne registers were searched for the children of the above marriages and for the burial of their parents. It is noteworthy that Carthew marriages were solemnised at Camborne in 1583 and 1588. They may have been, and probably were, those of John Carthowe's children.

been flowing, when we meet with it in the sixteenth century, it is impossible to say. Its persistence in the first half of that century is not more noteworthy than its arrest in the second half.[1]

Brittany had become a French province in 1495 by the marriage of Anne, Duchess of Brittany, to Charles VIII. The tortuous foreign policy of Queen Elizabeth of England, no less than the political and religious complications of her protracted reign, could hardly have been favourable to Breton immigration. The reformed religion and the decline of the Cornish language have prevented a renewal of close relations between the two countries.

The mystery and miracle plays constituted another link between Cornwall and Brittany. Whether written in Cornish or Breton they could be understood by the inhabitants of both countries.

They were acted on both sides of the Channel in the open air. The subject matter—sacred history and religious biography—was the same for both. The trilogy called the Ordinalia, which, in three plays, covered roughly the same ground as the Old and New Testament, represents the Cornish treatment, by means of the Cornish language, of the mystery, which, in the fifteenth and sixteenth centuries, was common to western Europe. But the miracle play of *Beunans Meriasek*, the life of St. Meriasek, was Celtic in origin and treatment. The Cornish version, written by Dom Hadton, in 1504, had probably a Breton archetype. St. Meriasek or Meriadec, who shares with St. Martin the patronage of Camborne,

[1] As late, however, as 1599 we meet with Bretons at Redruth, who contributed handsomely to the subsidy of that year. Six may be noted in the St. Ives district in 1571, but none in 1593 or after that date (Lay Subsidies, 87 (218)).

was unquestionably a very important personage in Brittany. He gave his name to a trève of Plumergat, Pluvigner, Pluneret and Noyal-Pontivy:[1] he is the patron of Stival and of Plougasnou. He was also numbered among the early bishops of Vannes, though, according to M. Loth, mistakenly.[2]

It is significant that in the Cornish *Beunans Meriasek* his elevation to that see forms an important episode. This fact, of itself, would suggest a Breton origin for the play. Mr. Thurstan Peter has, on other grounds, arrived at the same conclusion.[3]

The mystery and miracle plays were still in vogue when Richard Carew wrote his *Survey of Cornwall.* There is no need to quote the well-known passage in which he describes the degradation of what had once been a valuable means of instruction, but which, in his day (1590), had become a questionable form of popular entertainment.

At St. Just-in-Penwith and Perranzabuloe the plain-an-gware, place of the play, is more or less carefully preserved. The populous district of Plain-angwarry in the parish of Redruth also reminds the inhabitants of the days of old and the years that are past. In more than one manorial extent, as, for example, in that of the manor of St. Buryan, the writer has found a tenement, described as Plain-angware, the site of which is now unknown. It is not improbable that every considerable Cornish parish had formerly a space reserved for the mystery and miracle play.

[1] The trève is described by Dom Gougaud as a parochial subdivision still recognised in certain cantons of Brittany (*Chrétientés*, p. 124).

[2] Loth's *Les Saints bretons*, pp. 92, 93.

[3] Peter, *Old Cornish Drama*, p. 34.

No attempts have hitherto been made to revive these plays in Cornwall.[1] A graduate of Missouri University, visiting the Plain-an-gware at St. Just, informed the writer that in New York, with the assistance of wealthy patrons, the Cornish plays had been successfully rendered by members of the University. In Brittany there has been of late years a notable revival of the mysteries on modern lines in the Breton language. Under the direction of an enlightened clergy, encouraged by eminent Celtic scholars, the plays are attracting the attention of many besides those for whom they have been written. The marked histrionic ability of the players, most, if not all, of them simple country folk, the atmosphere of reverent adoring faith, and of robust inspiring patriotism, the utter absence of anything like vanity or pretence, the intense reality of the Gospel story which, too often, in the case of ordinary Englishmen, has, under the soothing influence of an inimitable authorised version of the Holy Scriptures, become an idyllic, poetical and idealistic presentment of Scriptural truth, but which, as proclaimed by the living voice and the impassioned fervour of believing hearts amid circumstances not very dissimilar to those which gave it birth: all this is irresistibly pathetic and convincing.

No one who has been present at St. Anne d'Auray and who has followed, even by means of a French translation, the Boéh-er-goèd (the Call of the Blood), in which the parable of the Prodigal Son is unfolded

[1] After the above was written, Mr. Thurstan Peter, President of the Royal Institution of Cornwall, announced that under the ægis of that institution the *Beunans Meriasek* would be performed in the year 1915. The great war has necessarily caused the postponement of the enterprise.

strictly on the lines of the sacred narrative, can ever forget it. In the words of Abbé le Bayon, the writer of the libretto, it is "par delà ce pauvre père qui souffrit un jour, dans quelque coin ignoré, de l'abandon inqualifiable de son fils—que chacun des spectateurs veuille bien entrevoir; le cœur de Dieu éternellement blessé des abandons humains; mais aussi, la vieille Bretagne toute déchirée au délaissement des siens et confiante encore, toujours aimante, rappelant à sa vieille langue, à ses croyances anciennes, les fils oublieux en qui repose l'espoir de la race." The appeal "à sa vieille langue" for Cornishmen comes too late, but that "à ses croyances anciennes" should meet with a response from those at least who are zealous for the traditions of their Cornish forefathers.

IV

THE CELTIC CHRISTIANITY OF CORNWALL

BY comparing the development of Christian institutions in the various portions of the Celtic world and observing those elements which were, for three centuries at least, characteristic, common and permanent, it ought to be possible to arrive at some very definite and useful results. It ought to be possible to supplement the evidence, supplied by writers like Gildas and the venerable Bede, and, from the common store of Celtic learning, acquired in Wales, Ireland and Brittany, to remedy our defective knowledge of Cornwall and of Cornish Christianity. Obviously the closer the relations between the four Celtic families the stronger the presumption in favour of an identity of ecclesiastical organisation.

Until the Saxon raids, which began in the year 428, Cornwall and Wales were integral portions of Great Britain ; the inhabitants, though differentiated into kingdoms, were bound together by a common religion and by a more or less common language.

The Roman occupation which in Armorica had changed the vernacular from Gaulish to Latin (which in the fifth century was, in that country, already giving rise to a romance language) achieved no such marked result in Britain. Latin may have been spoken in the centres of population and in places where the

Roman influence was exceptionally strong; it may have been spoken, as Professor Haverfield contends, in the eastern counties; but the absence of any trace of a romance language goes to prove that it was never the vernacular.

The Saxon invasion which, during the fifth and sixth centuries, reduced the Britons to a state of servitude, or drove them to the more inaccessible and remote regions of Wales and Cornwall, was the immediate cause of a great exodus to Armorica. No event in British history proved more fruitful in results: no event is more suggestive for the purpose of elucidating Cornish Church history. How large was the share taken in that emigration by the people of Dumnonia (Cornwall, Devon, Dorset and Somerset) may be gathered from the fact that the language which the emigrants introduced into Armorica—a language which speedily superseded Latin just as Latin had superseded Gaulish—was Cornish rather than Welsh, the language, in short, which survived in some parts of Cornwall until the eighteenth century and which is, with some slight modification, still spoken in Finistère and to some extent in Morbihan and Côtes du Nord. Professor Loth, whose eminence as a Celtic scholar no one will dispute, has written, "it is certain that linguistically the Britons of Cornwall were nearer of kin to the emigrants than the Welsh: they doubtless occupied the nearer neighbourhood of ancient Dumnonia." "The Breton language forms with Cornish a closely compacted unity as opposed to Welsh, although the three languages were assuredly very near neighbours at this period" (the fifth century).[1]

[1] *Les Noms des Saints bretons*, p. 143.

Armorica itself became known as Brittany in the sixth century. Cornwall (Cornouaille) was adopted as the name of that portion of it between the Elorn and the Ellé soon afterwards. Dumnonia was the name given to the northern portion between the Elorn and the Cuesnon in the ninth century. The settlers in Armorica introduced their own form of Christianity, and the object of the British and Irish missionary saints who flocked thither soon afterwards was not, as ancient writers have supposed, in order to convert the pagan Gauls, but rather to administer to the spiritual needs of their compatriots. To these missions our Dumnonia contributed little in comparison with Wales. Cornwall after the foundation of the kingdom of Wessex in 519 became isolated: its relations with Brittany were doubtless closer than with Saxonised Britain. But it never became, like Wales and Ireland in the fifth and sixth centuries, a great missionary centre. The founders of the Breton monastery-bishoprics—Pol Aurelian, Lunaire, Magloire, Mewan and Malo were all Welsh: Tutwal only, the founder of Tréguier, was of British Dumnonia. Of the British saints whose names are found in the parishes, fractions of parishes and holy places of Brittany, from 80 to 90 are Welsh; about 60 appear in Cornwall; from 30 to 40 appear only in Brittany and in Cornwall and Devon, and a few in Somerset.[1]

The British refugees remind us of Æneas whom tradition represents as bringing with him his Lares and Penates to Italy. The Dumnonian immigrants brought with them the cult of their own insular saints. At a later period Brittany was able to make a return in kind. Pol Aurelian, Sampson, Columba,

[1] Loth, *ibid.*, p. 124, n. 1.

Meriadec, Corentin and others of Breton fame were received into the devotional system of Cornwall.

Not only were the Breton and Cornish people one in origin, tradition, language and religious sentiment, they were one in their Celtic ideal of the priestly and religious life. Theirs no less than that of the Welsh and Irish was the monastic ideal. Every Cornish place-name bearing the prefix *lan*, together with some place-names bearing the prefix *nan*, implies a monastic foundation. Lanisley, Landithy, Lanhydrock, Lanherne and Landegy, Nancekuke and Nansladron are a few examples which show that the quasi-monastic foundations of Domesday Book were only modified survivals of what was in the sixth century the accepted ecclesiastical type, a type which continued to exist apparently long after the parochial system made its appearance. A body of celibate clergy, living in community, observing a religious rule and entrusted with the care of souls over an ill-defined area will probably represent the normal, just as an anchorite living solitary with a view to the perfecting of his soul in holiness will represent the abnormal development of the monastic ideal. We have no means of estimating the number of monks whose segregation constituted a Cornish lan. It is probable that the communities were small as compared with those of Wales and Ireland. The great monastery of Bangor Iscoed on the Dee had, according to the Venerable Bede, at the beginning of the seventh century no less than 2100 monks. Clonard, in the county of Meath, founded by St. Finnian about the year 520, is said to have been larger. It may be extravagance on the part of the biographer of St. Patrick to state that the saint enjoined a levy of a tithe of the men as well as a tithe of the land for the support of the Church,[1] but there can be no doubt that a very considerable fraction of the Celtic population embraced the religious life. At the same time we shall probably arrive at a false economic inference unless we bear in mind the tripartite division of the monk's day which required one-third of it to be spent in manual labour.

Professor Loth, as the result of a careful study of Breton toponomastic, has arrived at the conclusion that the Armorican parishes were placed as early as the sixth and seventh century under the invocation of the saints—national, emigrant, or otherwise—whose names they still bear.[2] It is therefore possible, I think probable, that the Cornish parish is older than the English. The reforms of Archbishop Theodore (668–690) which resulted in the subdivision of dioceses and the formation of parishes, were begun though not completed a little less than a century later. Cornwall and Wales were unaffected by these reforms, the Archbishop of Canterbury's jurisdiction not being acknowledged by Cornwall until the days of Egbert (803–839), or by Wales until the beginning of the twelfth century.

In the absence of clear historical evidence it would be rash to assert that every development in Wales, Brittany and Ireland was followed by a corresponding development in Cornwall, but where the same religious influences were at work in every other Celtic-speaking country it may be assumed that those influences were at work in Cornwall, and the receptivity of the Cornish in the matter of religion, when the influence was held

[1] Quoted by Dom Gougaud, *Les Chrétientés celtiques*, p. 82.

[2] Gougaud, *ibid.*, p. 107.

to come from the right quarter, is witnessed by the readiness wherewith they admitted Welsh, Irish and Breton saints into their hagiologies.

At the time under discussion it will be borne in mind that the saints reverenced in Cornwall were almost if not wholly Celtic. Even at the present time, in spite of the Saxon conquest and the submission to Canterbury, in spite of the attempt to substitute saints from the Roman Kalendar for the Celtic patrons of Cornish churches in the fourteenth century, and in spite of the ignorant perversion of spelling and the abortive attempts at identification on the part of the English registrars who conducted the business of the bishop's court at Exeter, it is a matter for wonder and gratitude that so many Cornish churches should still be known by their ancient saints' names.

If we compare the dedications of Derbyshire with those of Cornwall we find that of the 168 ancient churches in the former county, 72 are under the invocation of Scriptural saints, 18 under St. Michael, 28 under All Saints, 34 under historical saints like Martin, Lawrence and Giles and about 16 under English and Saxonised saints, like Edmund, Oswald, Wilfrid, Werburgh and Cuthbert.

On the other hand, in Cornwall, of the 200 dedications 30 are Scriptural, less than 30 are strangers (either historical and non-English like Martin, German and Clement, or aggressively English, like Morwenna, Werburgh, Swithun and Neot, or Saxonised like Cuthbert, Olave, Odulph and Hugh) and the rest, more than two-thirds of the total number, are Celtic. Nor is it difficult to account for the presence of the Saxon element. The monastic ideal presented by Werburgh the abbess and by Cuthbert the abbot-bishop would appeal to the prevailing monastic temper, while the early settlement of Saxons in the north-eastern portion of the county, of which we have abundant proof in its toponomastic (e.g. in Morwenstow, Jacobstow, Aldestow and Neotstou) and in the will of King Alfred (871–901) whose possessions in Triconshire (the hundred of Trigg which at that time probably embraced the hundred of Stratton) are expressly mentioned, will account for saints like Neot, Swithun and Morwenna who probably displaced the Celtic saints of an earlier period.

Before passing to what is of greatest interest—the Celtic episcopate—a few words are required respecting the two great controversies, which, however trivial in themselves, served the purpose of furnishing records of a period concerning which records are very scarce.

The Easter no less than the Tonsure controversy was one of the results of the isolation of Celtic Christianity. In order to find Easter the Roman Church had, until the year 457, used the old Jewish cycle of 84 years. In that year a cycle of 532 years was adopted. The Welsh and Cornish, who had received their Christianity during the Roman occupation of Great Britain, and therefore long before 457, continued to use the Jewish cycle. They refused to conform to the Roman use and persisted in their refusal for a very considerable period. Ireland, which had also become Christian before 457, was the first to adopt the Roman Easter in 633. Cornwall followed in or about 705, as the result of St. Aldhelm's famous letter to Geruntius, prince of Dumnonia. North Wales held out until 768 and South Wales until 777.[1]

[1] Haddan and Stubbs, *Councils*, etc., i, 201.

Mr. Haddan, who identifies the "errores" of bishop Leofric's Missal (909) with the "egregium errorem Brittonum" of Bede's history, is inclined to the opinion that St. Aldhelm's letter was inoperative outside the Kingdom of Wessex;[1] but the opinion is open to dispute.

The shaving of the head does not appear to have been associated with the Christian ministry until the fourth century. The apostolic injunction respecting long hair was observed, but it was the monks who introduced the tonsure which, at first, was a tonsure of the entire head and known as that of St. Paul. St. Peter's tonsure, which allowed to the shaven ecclesiastic an aureole or crown of hair around the denuded pate, was not introduced until the sixth century. Long before this time, however, the monks of the Celtic world had become distinguished by a tonsure which apparently made bare the fore part only of the head and left a semicircular fringe in front. The Celtic tonsure was taken by the British refugees to Brittany and Galicia. It was as characteristic of the Celtic clergy as the kilt is characteristic of Scottish soldiers to-day. Its origin was almost certainly Druidical, and, if so, it is one of the few shreds of evidence we possess of the presence of Druids in Cornwall. Their presence in Great Britain at an earlier period is generally allowed; their presence and power in Ireland is conclusively proved.

The Celtic tonsure appears to have been abandoned at the time when the Roman Easter was accepted.

[1] *Ibid.*, i, 674 and 676.

V

THE MONASTERY-BISHOPRICS OF CORNWALL

THE chief interest of Celtic Christianity gathers around the monastery-bishopric and the abbot-bishop who ruled it. In the sixth century the religious life had become much more than a counsel of perfection. In Ireland the Church was almost exclusively monastic. In Wales St. German is said to have founded a monastery during his second visit. Iltut, whom he ordained priest, was the founder of Llantwit, the great school of monks whence came Sampson, Paul Aurelian and possibly Gildas and David.

At the outset it is necessary to guard against the undercurrent of thought which connects Celtic monasticism with one or other of the great religious orders. The earliest of these orders—that of St. Benedict—was not established until about A.D. 529, and was not introduced into Britain until St. Augustine's arrival in A.D. 597. At the interview between Augustine and the Welsh bishops in 603 Dinoot abbot of Bangor Iscoed was among the strongest opponents of compromise. Celtic monasticism owed nothing to St. Benedict or to St. Augustine. When therefore we read the statement of a shrewd and learned writer like Sir John Maclean that " St. Petrock founded his monastery at Bodmin adopting the rule of St. Benedict" and when we recall an admission by the same writer that Petrock was educated at the great monastery of Clonard towards the end of the fifth or at the beginning of the sixth century, i.e. presumably between 490 and A.D. 510 and therefore before the Benedictine order was founded, we realise how mischievous this undercurrent of thought may prove.

There is no evidence that any early monastic foundation in the Celtic world was established in accordance with the Benedictine discipline. Celtic monasticism was quite definitely *sui generis.* The mission of St. German in 429 and 447 probably laid the foundations of it in Britain.

It had achieved some of its greatest victories before St. Augustine of Canterbury was born. Paul Aurelian, the Welsh monk, established the monastery-bishopric of Léon in A.D. 530: Sampson, a compatriot, the similar foundation at Dol in A.D. 565: Tutwal of British Dumnonia was abbot before he became abbot-bishop of Tréguier in the same century. In Ireland the monastery of Clonard was founded before the Benedictine order came into existence. St. Patrick was a contemporary of St. German. Celtic Christianity, while it was practically independent of Rome,[1] became intensely monastic. There is nothing therefore to lead us to regard the canons of St. Petrock, St. Piran, St. Stephen, St. Keverne and St. Probus, mentioned in Domesday Book, as subject to the discipline of St. Benedict. Such

[1] Cornwall's independence of Rome implied neither repudiation of nor secession from the Roman Church. It was merely the temporary suspension of outward communion with Latin Christianity as the result of political events which had placed Cornwall in a state of isolation.

evidence as we possess tends to confirm the contrary opinion. What has been said of the order of St. Benedict applies with greater force to that of St. Augustine, the Black Canons, whose earliest foundation in England dates from A.D. 1108, that is, 22 years after Domesday Book was compiled. Cardinal Gasquet truly says the clergy of every large church, as being subject to rule, were called canons. The rule of St. Augustine was not introduced at Bodmin until the time of Bishop William Warelwast (1107–36).[1]

Under the strong pressure exerted by monastic expansion the governmental character of episcopacy became attenuated. This was especially the case in Ireland and in those churches which owed their foundation to Irish missions. The multiplication of bishops tended to degrade the office. It is impossible to read the accounts of monastic rule as developed by St. Bridget at Kildare and by the Irish mission at Iona, and of the mechanical and subsidiary part which the bishops were called upon to play in the

[1] The statement is based upon the assumption that the decrees of Pope Leo III were as inoperative in Cornwall as they were in Wales and Ireland. It should be needless to warn the reader against confounding Augustine of Canterbury with the bishop of Hippo. The latter is said to have sanctioned certain regulations for the religious life which subsequently became known as the rule of St. Augustine. In the beginning of the ninth century Popè Leo III made this rule obligatory upon all the clergy who had not embraced some other rule. Had the monks of St. Petrock been in outward communion with western Christendom they would probably have become canons, regular or secular, of St. Augustine and, in that case and in that sense only, Sir John Maclean's statement might have been excusable. But in that sense the words had no meaning in the sixth century when St. Petrock founded the Cornish community. Augustine of Canterbury was a Benedictine monk and the canons regular introduced by Bishop Warelwast, known as Black Canons, belonged to one of the three great orders which sprang from the rule attributed to his great namesake the bishop of Hippo.

drama, without being aware of the subversion of one of the fundamental marks of episcopacy. The present writer has found but slight evidence of this disastrous policy in Wales and Brittany. There the abbot-bishop is seen as the ruler of a monastery or of a tribe. Innumerable monasteries had no bishop at all. The presence of a bishop gave to the monastery the elements of permanence and priority. The Breton and Welsh monastery-bishoprics have in many instances survived as bishoprics up to the present time solely, as it would seem, owing to their early episcopal character.

The distinction between the Irish and British conception of episcopacy must be borne in mind when we attempt to reconstruct the ecclesiastical institutions of Cornwall. It has been shown that the relation between Cornwall and Brittany was that of mother and daughter. Between Wales and Cornwall the relation, though probably less close, was far closer than that between Ireland and Cornwall. It is therefore more than probable that while the abbot-bishop was everywhere a distinguishing feature of Celtic Christianity there was here (in this county) no such perversion of the episcopal office as to give rise to a body of *episcopi vagantes* of whom we read in connection with Ireland and Irish missions.[1]

That Cornwall possessed bishops is certain, and that they ruled monasteries is equally certain, diocesan bishops being, during the period under consideration, practically unknown to the Celtic world. History helps us little as regards Cornwall. We know that in A.D. 664 two British bishops (duobus

[1] Dom Gougaud speaks of them as *Évêques déclassés et errants Chrétientés*, p. 219).

de Brittonum gente episcopis), whom Mr. Haddan considers to have been Cornish, assisted Wini, the Saxon bishop of Wessex, in the consecration of St. Chad.[1]

Gildas, the Jeremiah of Britain, whose *De Excidio* is stated to have been written in the sixth century, introduces us to an ecclesiastical system which, in respect of its main features, differs hardly if at all from that with which we are familiar, but which both surprises us by the evidence of its progress and alarms us by the extent of its perverseness. Gildas speaks of the clergy "intruding themselves into the preferments of the Church, yea, rather buying the same at a high rate" and "after the example of Simon Magus buying the office of a bishop or of a priest." There was, therefore, already in the sixth century, if the traditional date of the *De Excidio* be accepted, a gradation not only of dignity but also of office and emolument, for which, without Gildas' evidence, we should hardly have been prepared. The denunciations of Gildas have been held to apply to the civil rulers and the secular clergy only,[2] but there seems to be no good reason for accepting this hypothesis unless we read into the sixth century conditions which are found at a later period. It is important and sufficient for us to know that the British Church was highly organised and comparatively wealthy at this time.

To suppose, however, that Celtic monasteries were large, solid structures of stone with cloisters, refectories, dortors and the like is to mistake the economic conditions of the period and of the countries under

[1] Haddan and Stubbs, *Councils*, I, 124.

[2] Gougaud, *Chrétientés*, p. 67.

review. To associate the Celtic bishop with a durable and spacious cathedral church is almost as grotesque an anachronism as to represent St. Lucy (who died in the year 303), as they do in the sailors' church at Naples, apparelled in a modern court dress with a tiara of gems and a necklace of beautiful pearls.

The Celtic monastery has been compared to a pioneer settlement. It consisted of a congeries of detached cells, each suitable for the habitation of one or more monks. The cells, like the churches of the period, were commonly of wood, sometimes of stone. It is therefore, after the lapse of so many centuries, usually futile to seek for traces of them. Of existing Christian remains of the Celtic period in Cornwall the most noteworthy and interesting are the granite crosses and those monuments especially which bear the Chi-rho monogram. The chapels at Perranzabuloe, at Gwithian and at Madron are also of this date, the two former probably owing their preservation to the sand which buried them and the latter to the healing virtues of the waters of the holy well which flow through it.[1]

Having shown that the Celtic conception of episcopal jurisdiction was definitely monastic, as opposed to the Roman which, at an early period, had become diocesan, it is necessary to fix approximately the date at which, in Cornwall, the former gave place to the latter. Upon the solution of the problem depends the character to be assigned to the four Celtic bishops, Kenstec, Conan, Daniel and Comoere, whose names are disclosed in certain authentic documents and are given in the Truro Diocesan Kalendar.

[1] To this period Mr. Jenner would also assign the dwellings at Chysauster which may indeed, as he suggests, have been St. Gulval's nunnery.

In Brittany, a more progressive country and less isolated than Cornwall, the change was violently effected by the patriot Nominoë in the year 849. In Ireland the diocesan system was not adopted until 1152.[1] Wales submitted to the jurisdiction and discipline of Canterbury in 1207. It is certain, therefore, that Cornwall, more opposed to Saxon influence than any of the others, did not accept the diocesan system until the days of Egbert (836). There is good reason to believe that the change took place much later. Kenstec's letter to Archbishop Ceolnoth (833–870) states explicitly that his bishopric was monastic (*Ego Kenstec* . . . [ad] *episcopalem sedem in gente Cornubia in monasterio quod lingua Brettonum appellatur Dinuurin electus, etc.*).[2]

The next bit of historical evidence is that of Asser, the adviser of King Alfred, to whom Alfred in 884 committed Exeter *cum omni parochia quae ad se pertinebat in Saxonia et in Cornubia.*[3] The precise nature of the commission is uncertain. If the gift was made after Asser became bishop of Sherborne it probably involved the oversight of Devon and of that portion of Trigg, in Cornwall, where Alfred's possessions were situated. There is nothing to lead us to conclude that the Celtic Christianity of Cornwall was to be affected by it.

A very distinct advance, in intention if not in achievement, was made when, in 909, Archbishop Plegmund constituted the see of Crediton. To Eadulf the bishop were given three vills in Cornwall,—" Pollton, Coelling and Landuuithan from which

[1] Stokes, *Ireland and the Celtic Church*, p. 347.

[2] Haddan and Stubbs, *Councils*, I, 675.

[3] *Ibid.*, I, 676.

year by year he might visit the Cornish people in order to extirpate their errors. For in times past, as far as possible, they resisted the truth and were not obedient to the apostolical decrees." Pollton and Landuuithan are unquestionably Pawton in St. Breock and Lawhitton. Coelling presents some difficulty because Domesday Book and all subsequent records represent Callington (with which it has been identified) as ancient demesne of the Crown. It is possible, however, that before the Norman Conquest Coelling may have been surrendered to the King or have been exchanged for another holding.[1]

How far Eadulf was successful it is again impossible to say. A conquered race does not readily surrender its traditional religious customs. One of the most instructive records of the Jewish captivity is that which preserves the pedigrees of the priests who were themselves to preserve and perpetuate the priestly succession.[2]

Athelstan's policy (925–940) of excluding the Cornish from Exeter and confining them within the limits of their own province does not at first sight point to improved relations between the two races. His conquest of the whole of Cornwall may be accepted as fact and also his grant of lands to the church of St. Buryan. Perhaps the most important act of his life, so far as Cornwall was concerned, was, in the words of Leland, "to set up one Conan to be bishop in the church of St. German." The statement, even if copied from what he regarded as a trustworthy document, would have carried little weight

[1] It is even possible that Coelling may be Callestock in Perranzabuloe. The canons of Exeter had lands in that parish in the twelfth century.

[2] Ezra VII; Nehemiah XII.

as coming from a writer who lived 600 years after the event, had not Bishop Conan been found signing charters, undoubtedly authentic, between the years 931 and 934. Moreover, the name Conan is Celtic and occurs frequently in Cornish place-names. I am inclined to think that the Bishop Donan whose name is appended to the St. Buryan charter is a transcriber's mistake for Bishop Conan.[1] The question naturally suggests itself, how was it possible for a people smarting under recent defeat to accept the religious ministrations provided by their conqueror? Close upon a century had elapsed since the decisive battle of Hengestisdun, and during the interval doubtless a considerable portion of the Cornish had come to accept the Saxon supremacy. Athelstan's mission may have been, generally speaking, pacific though involving punishment to the disaffected and rebellious.

In choosing a Cornishman, and one probably already a bishop, for the see of St. Germans, he would be acting in a conciliatory spirit, especially if he, at the same time, recognised the traditional type of Cornish Christianity. There is no reason to interpret his action as involving a departure from it.

An interesting note is given by Haddan and Stubbs[2] which calls attention to the signature of one Mancant, a bishop, to a charter of 932 to which also Bishop Conan's name is appended. The learned editors rightly conjecture that Mancant was a Cornish bishop (Mancant, or more correctly Maucant). Coeval

[1] Donan, however, is a Celtic name (see Loth, *Rev. Celt.*, XXIX, 277). For the purpose of the argument which is here put forward it would have been more convenient to have distinguished between them.

[2] *Councils*, I, 979.

Cornish bishops are just what we should expect to find in the tenth century no less than in the sixth.

Quite the most valuable extant document of Cornish Christianity, however, is the List of *Manumissions on the Bodmin Gospels* which dates from the year 942 and carries us almost to the middle of the eleventh century. From this precious manuscript we gather that there were during that period the following bishops in, or connected with, Cornwall: (1) Athelgea[rd] possibly bishop of Crediton, (2) Comoere contemporary with Edgar (958–975), (3) Wulfsige of a slightly subsequent date, (4) Burthwold mentioned in Cnut's charter and described by William of Malmesbury as uncle of Living or Lyfing the penultimate bishop of Crediton. Charters also disclose two additional bishops: Ealdred (993–997) and Aethelred (1001). Of these Comoere, Wulfsige and Ealdred are identified by Mr. Haddan with Bodmin and Burthwold with St. Germans. Comoere's name is Celtic; the rest of the names are Saxon. But the important point is that they are all, except possibly the first, contemporary with, though not identical with, bishops of Crediton, in other words, some measure of independence continued to exist between the Saxon see and the see or sees of Cornwall. There is nothing to show that, before the days of Wulfsige (967), i.e. until within 80 years of Leofric, the first bishop of Exeter, the greater part of Cornwall was not Celtic both in religion and language. The change of ecclesiastical organisation was made at a period much later than is commonly supposed.[1]

[1] In the West of Cornwall there are indications in Domesday Book (1086) of the recent introduction of Saxon place-names, e.g. in Edward the Confessor's time it can hardly be a coincidence that Aluuarton (*hodie* Alverton) was the holding of Aluuar.

The charter of King Aethelred to Bishop Ealdred (994) seems to point to a period of transition. He gives to Bishop Ealdred episcopal jurisdiction in the province of Cornwall that it (the province ?) may be free and subject to him and his successors, "that he may govern and rule his diocese (*parochiam*) in the same way as other bishops who are in his realm, both the monastery (*locus*) and the domain (*regimen*) of St. Petrock being under the control of him and his successors." If the English conception of diocesan jurisdiction had been generally known and allowed in Cornwall there would have been no need to require the stipulations contained in the concluding paragraph. Ealdred was to administer the see of St. Petrock on English lines. History does not tell us what was, in the meanwhile, happening at St. Germans ; but twenty-four years later (in 1018) we meet with a grant of lands, in Landrake and Tiniel, by King Cnut to Burhwold bishop of St. Germans ; the Landrake lands were to be held by the bishop during his life and after his death they were to be held for the good of the souls of him and the King. The Tiniel lands were to be used as the bishop thought fit. It is interesting to note that these lands were not annexed to the bishopric but continued to be held by the prior of St. Germans until the dissolution of the priory in the sixteenth century.

At the time of Cnut's grant Cornwall had practically lost its independence both civil and ecclesiastical. All the witnesses of his charter, twenty-seven in number, bear Saxon names.

Burhwold died in or about A.D. 1043. Lyfing his nephew, who had become bishop of Crediton in 1027, was, in pursuance of an arrangement made long before between him and King Cnut, allowed to hold both sees. On Lyfing's death, in the third year of the Confessor's reign (1046), Leofric the King's chaplain was appointed to the united bishopric (*episcopatum Cridionensis ecclesiae atque Cornubiensis provinciae*) and the see transferred to Exeter. Papal sanction was obtained for the transaction three years afterwards.

By his charter of ratification, dated 1050, Edward the Confessor transfers the Cornish diocese which had formerly been assigned to a bishop's see (*episcopali solio*) in memory of Blessed German and in veneration of Petrock, this, with all parishes, lands, etc., he transfers to St. Peter in the city of Exeter. The absence of clear definition in the last paragraph is sufficiently obvious: no clearer definition was possible. There had been hitherto no Cornish diocese in the English and Roman acceptation of the word. There had been bishops both at Bodmin and at St. Germans within living memory holding lands and exercising jurisdiction, but the monastic tie was still probably stronger than the diocesan.

Yet it was obviously important, now that Exeter was to be the seat of ecclesiastical government for the two counties, that ample provision should be made for the great bishop who was to occupy it. Exeter lacked lands, books and almost every church ornament; so stated Pope Leo in his letter to King Edward. Accordingly the King not only gave to it lands of his own but he provided for the transfer of all that could under any reasonable pretext be claimed for its support. In effect, he made it possible for the Exeter bishopric to derive nearly one-half of its entire revenue from Cornish monastic lands. But the endowment of the see of Exeter requires a chapter to itself.

VI

EVOLUTION OF THE DIOCESAN-BISHOPRIC FROM THE MONASTERY-BISHOPRICS OF CORNWALL

THE Roman and, consequently, the Saxon conception of episcopal government was territorial and diocesan; the Celtic conception was tribal and monastic. An ecclesiastical system based upon tribal and monastic principles, recognising no supreme central authority, can afford to dispense with clearly defined boundaries. At the same time a monastic, no less than a tribal organisation, requires a centre of its own, towards which its activities may converge, and from which its influences may radiate.

The present is an attempt to show where the more important of such centres existed in Cornwall before diocesan was substituted for monastic rule. Doubtless every *lan* represented some such centre, however insignificant, just as every *caer* represented a fortified seat of civil authority. The *lan* justified its existence by the strength and fervour of its prayers and spiritual influence: the *caer* by the strength of its natural position and its artificial defences. A monastic settlement with a definite amount of demesne land, corresponding to its size and importance, upon which the monks worked for the support of the community, will sufficiently indicate what is meant. Some monasteries had bishops; some—the greater number—

were without them. The great monasteries of Landévennec in Brittany, Llantwit in Wales, and Bangor in Ireland, do not appear to have had bishops of their own, or, if they had, their episcopal character was submerged. On the other hand, the monastery-bishoprics of all three countries are too well known to require demonstration. The isolation of the Church in Cornwall until the middle of the tenth century encouraged and perpetuated the system in the mother country which in the fifth and sixth century it had helped to establish in Brittany.

Domesday Book, when studied by the light of earlier and later records, supplies invaluable information upon the subject of Cornish ecclesiastical organisation even before the Saxon conquest.

At the time of the Great Survey (1086), the bishop of Exeter held the following manors in Cornwall :

Treliuel (Treluswell in St. Gluvias).
Matela (Methleigh in St. Breage).
Tregel (Trewell in St. Feock).
Pauton (Pawton in St. Breock).
Berner (Burneir in Egloshayle).
St. German (St. Germans).
Lanherneu (Lanherne in Pydar).
Tinten (Tinten in St. Tudy).
Languititon (Lawhitton).
Landicla (Gulval).
St. Winnuc (St. Winnow).

Of these eleven manors all except five, viz. Burneir, Lanherne, Tinten, Lanisley, and St. Winnow, were demesne lands, the whole of their revenues going direct to the bishop. Richard Fitz Turold held Burneir and Tinten of the bishop, who received the profits of the former. Fulcard held Lanherne, and Godfrey St. Winnow. The services or profits rendered to the bishop in respect of four of the five manors would be comparatively trifling, except on the death of the tenant in demesne and during the minority of his heir. Consequently they are not considered worthy of mention in the *Taxatio*, made by Pope Nicholas IV of the bishop's temporalities in the year 1291.

In order to estimate the extent and value of the bishop's possessions in Cornwall it will suffice to compare them with those of the clergy, as given in the *Taxatio* or assessment just mentioned. It must, however, be remembered that Methleigh had ceased to be an episcopal manor before that assessment was made, having been granted by Bishop Robert Warelwast, between 1155 and 1161, to the dean and chapter of Exeter.[1] On the other hand, the manor of Cargol, in Newlyn, had been acquired in the meanwhile.[2] Moreover, Treluswell and Tregella, for civil purposes, had become differentiated into Camwerris (Penwerris), Trevella, Tolverne, Fentongollen, Trevennal, and Trelonk,[3] and for the purpose of ecclesiastical assessment had become known as Tregaher and Penryn.[4] In 1306 Tregaher, or Trocair, was the name of the major portion of the hundred of Powder, and was itself regarded as a hundred. The Bishop's holdings by military tenure in this hundred were rated at four knights' fees. Tregaher, the seat of these possessions, which lay east and west of the river Fal, is now known as Tregear in Gerrans. Roughly speaking, the bishop's manors in this district included the whole of the

[1] Inventory of Bp. Grandisson.
[2] *Exeter Episc. Registers, Stapeldon*, p. 97.
[3] Feudal Aids 1303, 1306, 1346.
[4] *Episc. Reg. Bronescombe*, App. p. 473.

parishes of Gerrans, St. Gluvias with Falmouth, Budock, Mabe, Mylor, Philleigh, Merther, St. Just-in-Roseland, and Ruan Lanyhorne. His demesne lands were very extensive and valuable, as will be seen by comparing the papal assessment of Tregaher (£20 11s. 5d.) with that of the rectory of Gerrans (£2 6s. 7d.) and the assessment of Penryn (£21 8s. 1d) with that of the benefice of St. Gluvias (£2).

Pawton and Burneir must be considered together, for they were doubtless both included in the grant made by King Edward the Elder to Eadulf when the see of Crediton was constituted in 909. The extent of the bishop's holding in Pawton at the time of the Domesday Survey (1086) is declared to be the entire hundred of Pawton, comprising 44 hides of land. It extended over the parishes of St. Breock, Egloshayle, St. Ervan, St. Eval, St. Issey, Little Petherick, St. Merryn, and Padstow. Pawton is only a contracted form of Petrockton, and there is sufficient reason to believe that these lands of the bishop had formerly belonged to the monastery of St. Petrock. In the Inquisitio Geldi (1085) the scribe appears to have found it difficult to describe the hundred of Pawton according to the prescribed formula. In his list of the hundreds he has interlined over "Rieltone Hundret" the words "Sci Petrochii,"[1] and has added Pauton at the end of the list. In his second attempt he has placed the hundred of Pauton first and omitted St. Petrock's altogether. It is interesting to observe that so late as the year 1691 the hundred

[1] St. Petrock's hundred had, of course, no connection with Rielton or Rillaton, subsequently known as the hundred of East. The confusion may have arisen from the fact that the bailiwick of Pydar was at Rialton, and that of East at Rillaton, formerly Rielton.

of Pydar is described in a grant from the Crown as "Petrockshire alias Pidershire alias the hundred of Pider." [1] Whether the word Pydershire is a sublimated equivalent of Petrockshire is a question for etymologists. That the two were not quite territorially conterminous is evident from Domesday Book itself, in which Nancekuke in Penwith and Forsnewth in West are included among the manors of St. Petrock. The important point to grasp is that out of the very heart of St. Petrock's province, Pawton, and with it what subsequently became known as the bishop's peculiar jurisdiction, embracing five parishes (*decanatus de Poltone*), was transferred in 909 from the monastery of St. Petrock to the new see of Crediton, and in 1046 to the see of Exeter. The episcopal revenue from Pawton in 1291 may be estimated by comparing its assessment (£49 16s. 3d.) with that of the church (appropriated rectory and vicarage) of Egloshayle (£5).

Lawhitton, given to Crediton at the same time as Pawton, was also of considerable extent. It consisted of eleven hides of land in 1086, and was assessed in 1291 at £25 10s. 11d., while the church or rectory of Lawhitton was assessed at £2. From what source it was obtained for the endowment of Crediton is not clear. Along with Lezant and South Petherwyn it was subsequently within the bishop of Exeter's peculiar jurisdiction. Possibly it had been taken (in 909) from the canons of St. Stephen near Launceston.

The manor of St. German, or, as it is called in the Exchequer Domesday, the manor of the church of St. German, consisted in 1086 of twenty-four hides

[1] Patent Roll, 3 William and Mary.

of land, the whole of which had been held by Bishop Leofric in the time of the Confessor. At the time of the Survey (1086) the bishop had twelve hides and the canons of St. German had twelve hides. The bishop had one hide in demesne, and the canons had one hide in demesne: the rest of the land was held by villeins either of the bishop or of the canons. It is clear, therefore, that between 1066 and 1086 a redistribution had taken place, as the result of which the bishop and the canons had been assigned equal shares of the lands. A Sunday market which had fallen to the latter had been reduced to nothing owing to a market on the same day having been established at Trematon Castle by the Count of Mortain. There had also been taken away by the Count from the church of St. German a hide of land which rendered as custom a cask (*cupa*) of ale and 30 pence, an acre (Cornish) of demesne land sufficient for one plough, and a virgate of demesne land which called for no remark. Of the usurped lands Reginald de Valletort held the two former, and Hamelin the latter, of the Count. In 1291 the bishop's manor of St. German was assessed at £17 16s. 5d., and the prior's holding at £14 13s. 4d. for lands in St. Germans, £1 for dues from South Petherwyn and Landulph, and £9 16s. 2d. for lands, including those of Tiniel and Landrake given to Bishop Burhwold by King Cnut in the year 1018. In the *Valor ecclesiasticus* (1535) to the revenues of the priory from the above sources there is added the impropriated tithe of Gulval, of which something more will be said when treating of Lanisley.

What actually happened shortly after the Norman Conquest in regard to St. Germans is not obscure, although some confusion has resulted owing to a misapprehension on the part of more than one writer Cnut's gift to Bishop Burhwold, as we have seen,[1] only served to augment the revenues of the religious community, of which Burhwold was doubtless the head. Under Lyfing, the nephew and successor of Burhwold, and before the death of Cnut, the see of St. Germans, such as it was, was united with that of Crediton, the community still consisting of secular canons. Leofric succeeded Lyfing, and in his days the see of Crediton and its possessions were transferred to Exeter. The revenue of St. German was consequently impoverished. Nothing appears to have been done to repair the loss until after Edward the Confessor's death, but, somewhere between 1066 and 1073, Leofric consented to a partition of the revenue by which the bishop and the canons became possessed of equal shares, as stated in Domesday Book.[2]

[1] See Monastery-Bishoprics, *supra*.

[2] The Patent Roll of 7 Richard II (cf. also *Monasticon*, edited by Oliver, p. 4) should be compared with the Patent Roll of 9 Richard II. The former states that Cnut was the founder of the priory of St. German, while the latter states that Leofric was the founder. Inasmuch as the charter of Cnut required the land of Landrake to be given after Burhwold's death to St. German for the good of the souls of Cnut and Burhwold (*Terram . . . commendat . . . Sancto Germano*) it follows that both statements were (and were probably understood to be) legal fictions. The earlier document, however, confirms, if confirmation were needed, the evidence as to the reconstruction of the monastery by Leofric as given in Domesday Book, though it is not necessarily conclusive as to the substitution of regular for secular canons. Preb. Hingeston Randolph (*Architec. Hist. of St. Germans*, p. 31) states that "there is no reason to suppose that Leofric took any steps to found a priory at St. Germans." The statement is far too sweeping. On the other hand, Mr. Haddan (*Councils*, etc., I, 704) relies upon the *ipsissima verba* of the Patent Roll for one of his main arguments for a single Cornish see in the days of Cnut. By itself the evidence supplied by an early patent roll relating to a transaction which took place nearly four centuries previously is not conclusive, especially when, as in this case, a legal title was needed in order to settle a dispute, and to place a bishop in undisputed possession of an advowson.

Having briefly reviewed the more important of the Cornish contributions to the revenue of the Exeter bishopric, a few words are required respecting the manors which, though absent from the *Taxatio* of 1291, were in 1086 amongst the possessions of the bishop, and were recorded in Domesday Book.

Matela or Methleigh, reckoned at a hide and a half in 1086, was granted by the bishop to the dean and chapter of Exeter, about the year 1160 and, by them, was conveyed soon afterwards to the family of Nansladron. It was to this manor that the church of St. Breage was appendant, and it may well have been the demesne land of a religious community before the Saxon invasion.

Landicla or Lanisley, also a hide and a half, was held by Rolland the archdeacon, of the bishop in 1086, having been Bishop Leofric's in the time of the Confessor. It embraced the whole parish of Gulval. Before the enactment of the statute *Quia emptores* in 1290, the whole of the demesne land appears to have been granted to the family of Fitz Ive. There is consequently no mention of it in the *Taxatio* of the following year, although the seignorial rights were subsequently claimed and exercised by the bishop from time to time as occasion arose. In 1580 it is described in an inquisition as having been held by John Tripcony of the bishop as of his manor of Penryn Foren, but the description, far from indicating a common origin of the two manors, probably only indicates a late expedient enabling the bishop to claim the services and collect the dues, if any, at his chief manor in the west. The advowson, and with it the rectorial tithe of Lanisley or Gulval, was at an early date held by the prior and canons of St. Germans, and continued to be held by them until the dissolution of their religious house in the sixteenth century. In the *Valor ecclesiasticus* their holding was assessed at £10 6s. 8d. It is not unlikely that when Bishop Leofric reconstituted the church of St. German he gave to it the advowson of Lanisley.[1]

Lanherne, the Lanherneu of Domesday, was a holding of Bishop Leofric before the Norman conquest, and was in 1086 held by Fulcard of the bishop. It was estimated at three hides. Of the incidents of tenure in subsequent times nothing remained to the bishop save homage, wardship, and the like, and the manor was not considered worthy of assessment in the *Taxatio* of 1291. It would be interesting to know how this manor came into the bishop's hands. It adjoined his manor or hundred of Pawton, and may have passed with it, but, curiously enough, the parish of St. Mawgan, with which it was almost conterminous, was not within the bishop's peculiar jurisdiction. The manor was, doubtless, St. Petrock's before it became the bishop's.

The manor of St. Winnuc or St. Winnow had already passed to a sub-tenant at the time of the Domesday Survey, and the impropriated tithe and advowson of the church of St. Winnow to the dean and chapter of Exeter, before 1291. There is nothing to suggest the source whence the manor was obtained for the endowment of the bishopric, save that St. Winnow

[1] There is a temptation to identify Lanisley with the Lannaledensis of the *Missa S. Germani* (Haddan and Stubbs, *Councils*, etc., I, 696). Alet, or Aleth, and Idles, in the parish of Kenwyn, are regarded as synonymous, if not identical, in several ancient charters. On the same principle Lanaleth would become Lanidles, a form sufficiently near that of Lanisle to convey the idea of identity. But Mr. Haddan is satisfied that Lanadleth is the British name of St. Germans, and the confusion introduced by the above supposition would be practically insurmountable.

adjoins Lanhydrock, which belonged to St. Petrock, and may, therefore, have been taken from the saint.

The manor of Tinten in St. Tudy, held in 1086 by Richard, of the bishop, was not considered worthy of separate mention in the *Taxatio* of 1291. It is the only episcopal manor the name or locality of which does not suggest an ecclesiastical origin. The advowson of St. Tudy was independent of it being appendant to the manor of Trethewell in St. Eval. Does the half hide of Tinten represent the lay contribution of Cornwall towards the endowment of the see of Exeter ?[1]

We are now in a position to summarise the results of the foregoing survey. We have seen that the Cornish possessions of the see of Exeter, at the time of the Domesday Survey, consisted chiefly of manors which had St. Germans, Lawhitton, Pawton and Penryn (or Tregear) for their centres. St. Germans and Pawton, and probably Lawhitton, were derived from monastic sources, viz. from the monasteries of St. German, St. Petrock, and probably from St. Stephen. The possessions in and around Penryn require further examination.

That there was a monastery-bishopric at Dinurrin or Dingerein in the ninth century is clear from Kenstec's profession of obedience to Archbishop Ceolnoth. To treat of Gerrans and its associations in an impartial spirit is wellnigh impossible. Legend, history and fact are so strangely and so suggestively interwoven that the temptation is equally great to say too much or too little. The name Gerrans is a modern form of Geraint or Geruntius. The presence

[1] Eglostudic (St. Tudy) and Polrode belonged to St. Petrock in the time of the Confessor, and Tinten may have been claimed for Exeter by virtue of the grant of 909.

of Gerrans, Just and Cuby, as the names of three churches and parishes near together, is indeed a remarkable coincidence if they are not identical with Geraint of Anglesey, his son Jestyn or Just, and his grandson Cuby, son of Selyf. No valid reason has been offered against the identification. Mr. Baring-Gould considers St. Gerrans the same person as Gerennius, King of Cornwall, who requested St. Teilo to visit and communicate him when dying (circa 556).

Both Geraint and Gerennius must be distinguished from Gerontius, prince of Dumnonia, to whom St. Aldhelm wrote at the request of an English synod in 705 urging him to abandon the Celtic method of determining Easter and the Celtic tonsure which the saint described as the tonsure of Simon Magus. All three (who are here distinguished as Geraint, Gerennius and Gerontius, though the names are identical) were historical personages and worthy of the veneration of after ages. For our present purpose it is not material to determine the identity of St. Gerrans : it is sufficient for us to know that Dingerein may be derived from any one of them. In the ninth century Dingerein or Dinurrin was the seat of the Abbot-bishop Kenstec. In the absence of evidence to the contrary we may suppose that his episcopate was concentrated at Gerrans and embraced the lands or parishes bordering the estuary of the Fal—those parishes in fact which subsequently became for ecclesiastical purposes the deanery of Penryn, and for civil purposes formed a large portion of the hundred of Trocayr or Tregeare. There is nothing to show that, either for ecclesiastical or for civil purposes, there were close relations, much less that there was a bond of union, between the Gerrans territory and that of Pawton, Pydar, St. German or Lawhitton. Gerrans was self-contained and independent. It may have retained, and probably did retain, traces of its episcopal character until Edward the Confessor, by charter, transferred the Cornish diocese with its lands and parishes to the see of Exeter. Some justification was doubtless required for the annexation of so much land in and around Gerrans to the bishop's demesne, and the only justification which is apparent is that it was already regarded as such.[1]

In the case of St. Gerrans hardly any trace was left of its monastic and episcopal associations. In the *Taxatio* of 1291 the benefice of St. Gerrans consisted of two portions, the rector's and the prior of St. Anthony's, which may point to a corporate life at an earlier date.

A glance at the map of Cornwall, in the light of what has been said, reveals, at the time of the Domesday Survey, present or past activities, on a considerable scale and monastic in character in every part of the county except in the north-east, and in the promontories of the Lizard and of the Land's End.

The north-east became Saxonised at a very early period. This is clear from the place-names. There is no reason to doubt that St. Neot, the Saxon monk of Glastonbury, settled in that part of Cornwall which bears his name, in the ninth century, and after founding a college of priests died, and was buried there. There is no reason to doubt the substantial accuracy of Asser's narrative—whether it be Asser's or another's

[1] At a much earlier date (670) St. Wilfrid claimed ecclesiastical endowments of the British for the Saxon Church in the neighbourhood of Ripon.

—which states that Alfred the Great hunted in the neighbourhood of St. Neot, and was healed, or believed himself to have been healed, at the shrine of St. Guerir. Alfred's possessions in Triconshire have been referred to. The community at St. Neot held two hides of land in the days of the Confessor, but the whole of it save one (Cornish) acre had been stolen by the Count of Mortain in 1086.

Again, the canons of St. Stephen-by-Launceston appear to have suffered a diminution of their power and also of their revenue owing to Saxon settlement. At the time of the Survey their affairs were in a state of utter confusion. They were attempting to hold on to lands which had been theirs, and are styled theirs in Domesday Book, which Harold held before the Norman Conquest, and which the Count of Mortain was striving to re-annex. In North-East Cornwall the Celtic type of Christianity had given place to the Saxon.

The promontory of the Lizard never became Saxonised. Everything here points to the persistence of the Celtic type and to very close and fruitful relations with Brittany. The names of the churches, including Manaccan, the monks' church,[1] are all to be found in Armorica except Grade (of very uncertain derivation) and St. Keverne. The word Meneage is itself possibly a derivative form of Manach. The lands given by the Count of Mortain to St. Michael's Mount, and described in his charter as situated in Amaneth,[2] were certainly in Meneage. Landivick, Langweath, Lantenning and, above all, Landewednack speak of monastic settlement. It is curious that the

[1] Loth, *Les Noms des Saints bretons*, p. 87.

[2] Amaneth may be an English equivalent for Anmanach. Treveneage appears at Trevanek in 1284, and as Trevanaek in 1361.

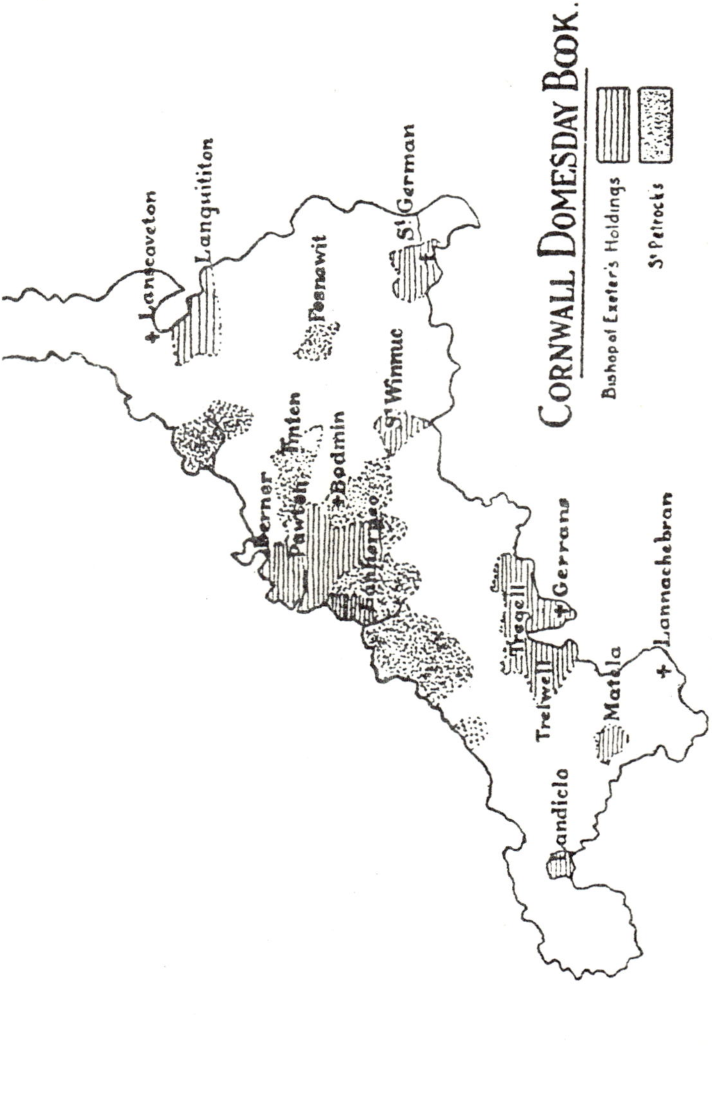
CORNWALL DOMESDAY BOOK.
Bishop of Exeter's Holdings
St Petrock's
Languititon
St German
St Winnuc
Bodmin
Pawton
Gerrans
Tregell
Trelwell
Matela
Lannachebran

Breton monastery of Landévennec and the church of Landewednack both claim Winwaloe for patron,[1] although St. Guenoc is possibly their true patron. However this may be, it is clear that a common influence has been at work in determining the nomenclature in both countries. In Domesday Book the hundred of Kerrier appears as Wineton or Winenton, the usual Saxon termination being added to a Celtic word as in Tedinton and Conarton. In later documents it is found as Winianton, and as such it remained until comparatively recent times, when it became Winnington. The point less than a mile west of Winianton is known as Pedngwinion. Mr. H. Jenner has suggested an interpretation which is almost certainly correct, viz. that Winianton means the home of the shining or blessed ones. Winianton, as the name of a hundred, implies some sort of local pre-eminence, past or present. Before the Norman Conquest the *manor* of Winianton embraced 22 sub-manors which were in the hands of 17 thegns. The description of these thegns is interesting—they could not be separated from the manor and they rendered custom in the same manor. Before 1086 they were supplanted by the Count of Mortain's men. A thegn, according to Professor Maitland, was, before the tenth century, " a household officer of some great man " and, from the tenth century until the Norman Conquest, a person socially above a churl with corresponding privileges and responsibilities.[2] Now it is remarkable that the thegns of Winenton differed in no respect from those of St. Petrock, except that whereas the former could not be separated from the

[1] Loth, *Les Noms des Saints bretons*, pp. 52, 53.

[2] *Hist. of English Law*, i, 33.

manor, the latter could not be separated from the saint.

Have we here the note of tragedy, inseparable from a lost cause, of which the Lizard district, to its lasting credit, furnished two other conspicuous examples in the sixteenth and seventeenth centuries ? It looks[1] as if there had been the overthrow of monkish supremacy by the Cornish, followed by Saxon Conquest, and in the meantime the preservation of thegnship until the Norman Conquest. The small community of St. Keverne despoiled by the Count of Mortain represents Irish influence, if we suppose with Mr. W. C. Borlase that Keverne is identical with Kieran. This saint is not found among the Breton dedications, Peran and Kerrien being regarded by Professor Loth as different saints, and neither of them identical with Keverne or Kieran. We, therefore, conclude that the agency which compassed the destruction of Brittonic monachism in Meneage left the Irish house to the tender mercies of the Norman invader. It is possible that in the church of St. Breage we have an attempt at reparation. From time immemorial it embraced Germoe, Cury, and Gunwalloe as chapelries. Methleigh, the only manor which escaped Norman rapacity as the result of its having been added to the Exeter bishopric, may have been originally a portion of the demesne of the monastic body which dominated the Lizard peninsula.

Respecting the hundred of Penwith, we have little historical evidence prior to the Norman Conquest. Athelstan's grant to the church of St. Buryan and Edward the Confessor's grant to St. Michael's Mount,

[1] The references are to Kilter's rising in 1549, and to the prolonged defence of Little Dennis by Sir Richard Vyvyan in 1646.

whatever fault may be found with the charters, as they have come down to us, are sufficiently authentic. The story of St. Ia's arrival with her Irish companions must be received with caution ; but there is no reason to doubt that a substratum of truth lies beneath a legend which is by no means modern. Seven churches in Penwith bear the names of these missionaries. On the other hand, no less than fourteen dedications, including two which subsequently became obsolete and two which are among those of the Irish mission, are common to Penwith and Brittany. The remaining dedications are of doubtful origin. It seems, therefore, certain that Irish and Breton influences had a great deal to do with the moulding of the church life of the hundred. The preponderating influence was Breton. The presence of St. Pol Aurelian (Paul) and of Winwaloe (Towednack) is sufficient evidence of this. It is remarkable that four, if not more, of the Penwith churches afford traces of presumably earlier dedications. St. Erth (possibly also Perranuthnoe) was known as Lanudno, Gulval as Lanisley, Madron probably as Landithy,[1] and Illogan probably as Lancichuc. St. Just may have borne the name of Lafrowda, as being situated near the holy springs. Udno (Goueznou) the companion of Pol Aurelian (circa 530) is commemorated in three Breton parishes. Pol was originally of Wales, and a contemporary of Just of Anglesey, who is probably the patron of the church which bears the name in Penwith. If this be so, St. Levan will be Seleven, Salomon, Selyf, or Selus, whose memorial stone is preserved in St. Just Church. It is quite possible that the changed dedica-

[1] The evidence is indirect. Trengwainton, to which the advowson was appendant, was itself a sub-manor of Roseworthy in Gwinear. Landithy is only a short distance from the church.

tions indicate a change from monastic to some sort of parochial organisation. In Penwith there does not appear to have been any monastic community of commanding importance whose revenues could be seized without leaving the people spiritually destitute. Lanisley may have been one which had outstayed its welcome and on that account may have become attached to what was eventually to become the see of Exeter.

To sum up. Three large holdings, or, to use a modern though inadequate word, estates, stand out clear and distinct, viz. those of Gerrans, Pawton and St. Germans, each of them at one time or another associated with the see of a Cornish bishop, monastic in character. Such records as we have, carefully distinguish these lands from one another. Neither St. Petrock (Pawton) nor St. German possesses any rights in Gerrans, nor Gerrans in Pawton or in St. Germans. Neither does St. Germans claim rights in Pawton, nor Pawton in St. Germans. It is not only opposed to the evidence of Domesday, it is inconceivable that any Cornish bishop exercised lordship over all three at the same time. The Pawton lands were almost certainly claimed by Crediton by virtue of the provision made in 909 for missionary visits to them yearly by the bishop of Crediton. The St. Germans holding was certainly annexed to Exeter when that see was founded. The Gerrans holding presents several difficulties. We have no record of any bishop at Gerrans save Kenstec (865). But because no records have been preserved, we cannot say that no bishops existed. Such a principle if applied to Cornish parishes would be fatal to their claim to have had a rector before the days of Bishop

Bronescombe (1257). Nevertheless, the absence of recorded evidence is distinctly embarrassing. What were the events or circumstances which justified the annexation of the Gerrans property to the see of Exeter? Some justification there doubtless was. Was it found in the letter of submission written by Bishop Kenstec to Archbishop Plegmund (833–870) about fifty years before the see of Crediton was founded? Was it found in the forfeiture of royal possessions consequent upon the conquest of Cornwall by Athelstan (925–940)? It is possible that both these events may have contributed to the result, for there is good reason to believe that Gerrans was a residence of the kings of Cornwall in the seventh century, and it is certain that it was the residence of Kenstec in the ninth century. If the lands were claimed by King Athelstan there ought to be some charter to show when and by whom they were transferred to the see of Crediton or of Exeter. If they passed to the Saxon bishopric by virtue of the grant of Edward the Confessor in 1050, then we must conclude that they had preserved their episcopal associations until within a few years of that time, and that, therefore, Bishop Kenstec probably had successors at Gerrans. It is inconceivable that there were not valid grounds for the transfer of the lands. The fact that they were monastic lands would not have sufficed, for the canons of St. Petrock and St. German survived the annexation of a portion of theirs, whereas no vestige of a monastery remained at Gerrans in the days of the Confessor. It was its former connection with episcopal rule which led to the inclusion of Gerrans in the endowments of the bishopric of Exeter.

The foregoing fragmentary sketch is not to be regarded as a conclusive proof of the existence of concurrent Cornish bishoprics so late as the eleventh century, but it is intended to call attention to some of the sources from which others may seek the necessary means of forming a judgment for themselves. That the monastery-bishoprics were hard to suppress will be evident to everyone who examines the evidence. That they survived in Cornwall for a much longer period than is generally supposed seems more than probable.

VII

CORNISH SAINTS

IN the first chapter it has been attempted to show how the tyranny of resemblance and coincidence leads to false analogies and wrong inferences. Some further illustrations of this principle which have a direct bearing upon the main purpose of the present enquiry may be found instructive.

In this chapter we are not so much concerned with the Lives of the Cornish Saints, as they have come down to us, as with the question whether they had any actual existence as human beings at all. Of Ia, Uny, Dennis, Allen, Paul and Berrian it has been stated that "it is more than probable that there was no man in either case. Ia is the Island saint, Uny the Downs saint, Dennis the Hill saint, Paul or Pol the Pool saint," Buryan or Berrian the saint of Berrie.

But why stop there? Domesday Book supplies us with Eglostudic, Sainguilant and Sainguinas. It is just as easy to imagine places bearing the names of Tudic, Guilant and Guinas as to imagine one bearing the name of Berrie, and quite as good etymology to derive them from Tutton a chair, Guilan a kingfisher and Guenan a blister.

Most will admit that a chair saint is suggestive of saintly pursuits—study and contemplation; many saints have been fishermen; some have suffered from pimples and perhaps have known how to cure them.

Again we have two more ancient parishes one of which occurs in Domesday Book, viz. Eglosros (Philleigh) and Egloshayle, the church on the heath and the church on the estuary, yet no one has ever ventured to describe or to speak of them as the churches of St. Rose and St. Hayle, and for the obvious reason that Cornish saints have not been manufactured in the way that has been suggested.

In choosing Ia, Uny, Dennis, Allen, Paul and Berrian to demonstrate his theory, the critic could hardly have made a more unfortunate selection. With one exception they are all to be found in Brittany.

Ia is said to have been an Irish missionary who came with her brothers Uny and Erth and some others to complete the conversion of the Cornish in the golden age of Celtic Christianity. For our present purpose it is not material to accept the legend, but it is useful to know that Ia is commemorated at St. Ives in Cornwall and in Finistère in Brittany, Erth at St. Erth in Cornwall and at Chittlehampton in Devon, Uny at Lelant and Redruth in Cornwall and at Plevin in Côtes du Nord. St. Dennis (or Denys), his church being situated in the centre of a hill-fort, is the only one whose name seems, at first sight, to lend colour to the new criticism. But to quote Professor Loth, writing on a totally different subject,[1] "it is quite impossible for Dinas by itself to be a man's name. It is one of the most widely distributed place-names in Cornwall. Dinas in Cornish, as in Welsh, signifies a fortified

[1] *Romans de la Table ronde*, p. 90.

town." Assuming that a personage derived his name from the place Dinas we should have Dinan as in Cardinan. St. Dennis or Denys appears to have been the name given to a chapelry of St. Stephen (Etienne) but there is no reason to suppose that it was ancient when it first appears along with that of Caerhayes in the *Inquisitio Nonarum* (1340) as *Capella Sci. Dionisii.* St. Denys, supposed, but mistakenly, to be identical with Dionysius the Areopagite, was from the seventh century onwards venerated throughout Europe, and it is not remarkable to find him the patron of a chapel in Cornwall in the fourteenth century.

That the name of the site of the chapel may have suggested to its founder a name for its patron saint is quite possible. As late as the seventeenth century the heralds chose St. John Baptist's head for the arms of Penzance (holy head). There are, in truth, no better grounds for regarding St. Dennis as mythical than St. Stephen to whom his chapel was appendant.

St. Allen, as the presiding saint of the *hail* or moor, reminds one of some rather irreverent lines by the greatest of Irish poets :

> Our preacher prays he may in'erit
> The hinspiration of the Spirit.
> Oh ! grant him also, 'oly Lord,
> The haspiration of thy word.

St. Allen is found as St. Alun in the Episcopal Registers. The name occurs in the cartulary of Redon and in Coed-Alun near Carnarvon in Wales. St. Alan is among the disciples of Iltut and is the patron of Corlay (Côtes du Nord). In no instance is the name found with the aspirate, or hail without it.

Pol de Leon is a personage quite as historic as Napoleon. It must rest with the reader to say whether the church in Cornwall which bears his name got it from Gwavas Lake or from the well-known British saint, a disciple of Tutwal, who founded a Breton bishopric, who was a fellow-student of St. Sampson the patron of Golant and who is himself the patron of fifteen parishes, one of which curiously enough is in Cornouaille in Brittany.

Eglosberria remains and this, we are told, is compounded of Eglos and a Cornish place-word presumed to be Berrie. The fact that no such place is now to be found in the parish of St. Buryan does not, of eourse, prove that in the far remote past there may not have been one. Nor does it concern us much to know that in the parish berries of sorts are abundant, holly berries, elder berries, blackberries and goose-berries ; still less to consider whether the last-named berry is indigenous or acclimatised. This is not a treatise on Botany.

Had our critic consulted his reference, Domesday Book, he would have read in the Exchequer redaction, " The Canons of St. Berriona hold Eglosberrie " ; in the Exeter book—the original document—under the heading Inquisitio Geldi (1085), " St. Berriana holds a hide of land " ; and under the heading Land of St. Berriona the Virgin, " the Canons of St. Berriona hold a manor which is called Eglosberria, which the same Virgin held in the time of King Edward freely " (i.e. free from the payment of dues). The first point to notice is that in every case the name of the saint is trisyllabic, Berrian or Berrion. Berria, the second half of the name of the manor, is probably only a contraction for Berriana made by the earlier scribe and copied by the later. This explanation is placed almost beyond dispute by earlier and later documents concerning the manor and the church. Again it is well known that the letters *b* and *v* are, in certain Cornish words, interchangeable as, for example, in Trebean and Trevean. Professor Loth had pointed out to the present writer that Berrian (Buryan) and Verrian (Veryan) were identical, but it was two years before a striking confirmation of his statement was disclosed. A charter dated 1450 was recently handed to me to decipher relating to this very manor of Eglosberrie.

In it the lands were described as those of Eglosveryan. The Domesday record is not only in perfect agreement with, but confirms, the charter of Athelstan, which, in spite of some adverse criticism, probably arising from the fact that it has been copied and attested more than once, is acknowledged to be a trustworthy document, and as such was always regarded whenever the rights and privileges of the royal chapel of St. Buryan were called in question. Veryan and Buryan being identical, it follows that, on the assumption that they are derived from Berrie, a place-name, that place will be found in both parishes. It is found in neither. It is purely mythical.

It may be asked, why devote so much space to a matter of secondary importance? The reason is that here we have to meet an attempt to bring the Celtic saints within the province of comparative mythology, an attempt to show that they were eponymous in somewhat the same sense as Romulus, Cypris, Pallas Athene and Ceres (as representing Siculus) were the genii and afterwards the presiding deities over Rome, Cyprus, Athens and Sicily. It is useless to deny the assertion that "the Church history of Cornwall before the Norman Conquest is chiefly a matter of legendary lore" and that "the cult of the sun was that of Cornwall not a thousand years ago" unless we have something to say in support of our denial.

Let us therefore carry the argument a little further —let us suppose that the topological origin of the saints is the true one; let us suppose that there is indisputable evidence, gathered in Cornwall, in its favour; in other words, that the Cornish saints are local divinities; how will it fare with them when their votaries have crossed the seas? Will the Island which gives its name to St. Ives, will the Downs of Lelant, the Hail (deprived of its aspirate), the Dinas of Mid-Cornwall and Gwavas Lake win Armorican devotion? Or conversely, assuming the saints to have been of Armorican manufacture, will they appeal to the devotional instincts of the Cornish? Or must we assume that there was a sacred island at Plouyé, a sacred downs at Plevin, a sacred pool at Léon and a sacred Berrie at Berrien and Lan-verrien in Finistère? It is as difficult to imagine an affirmative answer being returned to any of these questions as St. Thomas Aquinas found it to believe that a religious could tell a lie, and therefore, according to his biographer, more difficult to believe than that an ox could fly. The Celtic saints were not eponymous, but men of like passions with us, who lived their lives, told their story, impressed their contemporaries and were gathered to their fathers, men honoured in their generation and the glory of their times.

This leads to a brief notice of their biographies.

The subject is not free from difficulty. It requires a rearrangement of thoughts, a re-focussing of ideas. The Lives of the Saints do not conform to ordinary standards or respond to ordinary appeals.

They are not plain, unvarnished accounts of simple earnest men written by their contemporaries, but, in their present form, they are for the most part highly coloured stories addressed not to the intellect but to the imagination. They are not always free from anachronisms. The ideals of their writers are not ours to-day.

They abound in the miraculous. They are adorned after a common pattern peculiarly their own. They draw largely upon Holy Scripture. Incidents related of one saint are sometimes transferred to another. Similarities of expression are found in them, perhaps pointing to a common origin or authorship. In short, all the elements which provoke adverse criticism are found in them.

And yet, making due allowance for the mentality of those who wrote and those who read them, there is no sufficient reason for impugning the veracity of the writers, much less for despising them.[1] They were neither deceivers nor deceived. The hagiographer had probably as great a regard for truth as his modern critics, but he knew nothing of the canons of literary excellence. He had never heard of "nature unadorned"; but he knew, just as we

[1] To quote M. Loth, whose gentle irony would be spoiled by translation, in his answer to M. Fawtier's criticism: "Il (M. Fawtier) a été évidemment, d'avance, fâcheusement impressioné par le fait même d'avoir affaire à un *hagiographe et ce qui plus est*, comme il l'avoue sans détour *à un hagiographe breton.* Si nos hagiographes meritent une place d'honneur dans le martyrologe de la critique, c'est peut-être bien que nos vies de saints sont d'une assez basse époque: la vie de Samson mise à part, les deux plus anciennes ont été redigées vers la fin du ixe siècle."

know, how banal and commonplace are the lives of many of the best men and women who have lived and worked for others, and he strove to portray them in colours which might make them interesting to a generation whose intelligence, so far as religion was concerned, had been chiefly moulded by Holy Scripture. He recognised analogies and emphasised them. He was conversant with the main facts and knew how impressive had been the personality and the life of his hero, but he had not, like Boswell, followed him about with a note-book. He was himself an impressionist and by no means sparing of his paint, one whose work doubtless won the approval of the age in which he lived. He had no message for succeeding ages.

At the same time only ignorance or prejudice will place all hagiographers on the same level or refuse to take account of alleged facts, even when they are concealed underneath an intolerable deal of fanciful adornment.

In some cases the Lives of the Saints, as presented by their authors, possess real historical value. Those of Sampson, Paul Aurelian, Winwaloe, Tutwal and Malo (Machutus) fall within this category.[1] The life of St. Sampson drawn up, according to Mgr. Duchesne, towards the end of the seventh century, of which the earliest and most valuable MS. is of the eleventh century, will repay diligent study.[2] It has a direct and important bearing upon monastery-bishoprics, and ought to possess a special interest for

[1] J. Loth, *Revue Celtique*, xxii, p. 96.

[2] The text has been edited by M. Fawtier and published by MM. Champion (Paris). The reader should consult also the more critical notes on *S. Samson de Dol*, by Prof. Loth (Champion, Paris) and if possible a very illuminating little treatise, *La vie de S. Samson*, by M. L'Abbé Duine.

the people of Cornwall whose forefathers profited by St. Sampson's ministry. The biography, as we should expect, contains its full share of miracles, but is, nevertheless, characterised by veracity in those statements which relate to the saint's parentage, private life, travels and career. The picture is a true picture, however much we may dislike the method of treatment. The landing of the saint near Padstow, his sojourn at St. Kew, his destruction of the pagan idol in the hundred of Trigg and other details are all related and the topographical knowledge of the writer has been shown to be accurate.[1] It is doubtful, however, whether, at the present stage of historical research, it is possible for those, who are most competent to form a judgment of the value of the evidence afforded by the Lives of the Saints, to do so dispassionately and impartially owing to the antagonism which is provoked by the extraordinary play of fancy on the part of their writers.

That some of them possess historical value is proved by a Life the earliest MS. of which is comparatively recent. In the life of St. Petrock the text of which is not earlier than the fifteenth century it is stated that "Petrock, after visiting his compatriot St. Sampson, betook himself *ad cellam Wethnoci episcopi.* A little further on we read *unde etiam lingua gentis illius Landuuethmoch* (for Lannwethnoc) *adhuc usque hodie dicitur.* Now Lannwethnoc presents itself in Domesday Book under the forms of Lanwehenoc (wrongly written Lanwenahoc) and Lan-guihenoc."[2]

The remarkable thing is that a fifteenth-century

[1] Loth, *Saint Samson de Dol*, p. 26.

[2] See the previous footnote.

writer should have recorded two facts which were as little known at the time when he wrote as they are to the generality of English readers to-day; the first, that in the days of St. Petrock a bishop might have been found occupying a cell, living as a monk or hermit, though not necessarily living alone; and the second, that there was in pre-Norman times a place bearing the name of Languihenoc, both of which are placed beyond dispute by the evidence given us in the chapter on Monastery-Bishoprics and by the testimony of Domesday Book. It surely requires an imagination of wider scope to believe that the writer was not transcribing or interpreting an authentic document than to accept the most fantastic legends of Celtic saints. The service rendered to research is twofold: it witnesses to the historicity of the Life even if it does not establish the reputation of its writer, and it adds one more to our list of Celtic bishops in the person of Guethnoc, who as Gwethnoc is honoured in Finistère and elsewhere in Brittany.

At this point it seems convenient to summarise the results of our survey. It has been maintained that coincidence and resemblance have been invested with an importance disproportionate to their real value, that where coincidence has been claimed for the purpose of discrediting traditional doctrine it has often proved as illusory as the rainbow, that resemblance unsupported by other evidence has proved to be imaginary or superficial, that in the case of the Cornish saints, whose names have been supposed to resemble place-names, there is nothing to warrant the suspicion that they are eponymous, that the Lives of the Saints as they have come down to us must be estimated in the light of the mentality of the writers and readers of them, that, however ornate or barbaric they may be considered to be, when they record ordinary events the statements are worthy of investigation and often of historical value, and that a comparatively modern life of a saint may afford evidence of the substantial accuracy of the facts which it records.

It may not unreasonably be asked what then is the attitude to be observed towards those students of comparative mythology who endeavour to find a common origin for all religions by studying religious phenomena? There is no reason why it should not be friendly or even helpful. But, whatever may be the final verdict of that study, its present value will be generally determined by psychology rather than by logic. The man who starts with a theory, whether in favour of a common origin of religious belief or with one opposed to a common origin, will probably find enough evidence to confirm his theory. Darwins are not born every day; yet there is no hope which is more widely shared or more secretly cherished by those who give themselves to mythological research than the hope that they are at least potential Darwins. The desire to be scientific, that is, to reduce to system an array of facts, vastly preponderates over the desire to ascertain the accuracy of certain alleged facts and their relation to other facts of a similar nature. It is possible to accept the statement that worship originated in sacrifice, in the attempt to propitiate an offended deity, and to deduce conclusions diametrically opposed to each other. To the Catholic Christian it will perhaps be a substantial aid to faith, to the Protestant an encouragement to discard the errors of paganism, to the unbeliever a confirmation of unbelief. The subject—only as yet in its infancy—can hardly be ignored. At the same time its ramifications cover so much ground that comparatively few can be expected to acquire sufficient knowledge to be in a position to judge of its conclusions. Archæology, philology, ethnology, ancient philosophy, theology and mythology are only some of the departments of a study which aims at determining the origins of religious belief. Who then is sufficient for these things ? He has yet to be born.

Cornwall, with its large admixture of Celtic blood, until lately speaking a Celtic language, inheriting a Celtic tradition, for centuries in close contact with Brittany, might have been expected to furnish materials enabling the student to differentiate the quality of its religious belief and practice from that of the Midlands. To accept the same creed is not necessarily to hold the same belief or to have the same religious ideal. Each people has doubtless its own instinctive beliefs which may or may not find a place in the creed which is professed. If those beliefs do find a place in it they will find emphasised expression in the popular worship. The appeal of Wesley in the eighteenth century struck home to the instinctive beliefs of the Cornish. In spite of the marked progress of Anglicanism during the last half-century the Cornish are largely Methodists, whose worship is still conducted in buildings which usually have as little claim to beauty as a railway station. They have no stereotyped form of service, no liturgy which lends itself to musical adornment. The hospitals and other charitable institutions in the county have in many cases been built and are mainly supported by others. And yet the Cornish possess a keen sense of beauty. They are musical, refined and generous. In skill and intelligence they will bear comparison with the rest of the United Kingdom. They are open-minded, fond of discussion and never tired when it takes a religious turn. Their nearest kinsmen in blood are the Bretons, with whom they have much in common, although in the matter of religious practice they are as far as the poles apart. While the latter cling with unrivalled devotion to the old religion, the former spend much time, like the men of Athens, in telling or hearing some new thing. Methodism on the old lines is moribund in Cornwall; Catholicism on the old lines is a living and a growing power in Brittany. During the last quarter of a century a remarkable change has passed over the face of Cornish nonconformity. Revivals have almost become things of the past. Conversion, theoretically the starting-point of Methodist religion, is no longer required to be sudden. The class meeting has lost much of its attractiveness. There is less reverence for the Holy Scriptures. Many of the old doctrines are being recast. Methodism is in a state of transition. The drift is towards rationalism, but the end is not yet in sight. Under these circumstances it is not easy to form a right judgment or to forecast the future of Cornish Methodism, but to one who has spent twenty-five years in its midst and who knows how deeply and instinctively religious is the character of the people it would seem that at a no distant date there will be a *volte-face*, in other words, that the essentially religious instinct will reassert itself. Two alternatives may supervene. There may be a return to the Catholic faith, Anglican or Roman, of which there are already signs or there may be recourse to Christian Science, Spiritualism or some occult system which attracts by its novelty and promises to satisfy religious craving. Rationalism, which may suit the Teutonic race and be a substitute for religion, is impossible to the emotional God-fearing temper of the Celt.

VIII

ANCIENT RELIGIOUS HOUSES

A BRIEF survey of the monastic and quasi-monastic foundations is required in order to determine if possible which of them, if any, were originally Celtic in character. It will suffice to take the *Monasticon*, as edited by Dr. Oliver, and to examine the charters and notes respecting the several houses and to check them by means of such other records as are available. Neither Sir William Dugdale nor Dr. Oliver distinguished between institutions which were Celtic and institutions which were the common heritage of Western Christianity.

If a monastery existed before the Norman Conquest their main purpose was to trace it back, if possible, beyond that date, and, having done this, to record its fortunes as it fared forth through the centuries which followed. This purpose they achieved by printing in chronological order all its charters, whether preserved as chirographs or as inspeximi[1] derived from Charter and Patent Rolls. The following list

[1] Inspeximi is a convenient plural of the word *inspeximus* (we have inspected). Royal grants of liberties and privileges are frequently based upon earlier grants which the Royal grantor declares he has *inspected.* The charters of these earlier grants in many instances no longer exist.

comprises all the Cornish religious foundations given in the *Monasticon :*

St. Petrock's (Bodmin) Priory.
St. German's Priory.
St. Michael's (Mount) Priory.
St. Stephen's (Launceston) Priory.
St. Buryan Collegiate Church.
St. Crantock Collegiate Church.
St. Cyricus, or St. Cyriacus, Priory.
St. Probus Prebendal Church.
St. Keverne Collegiate Church.
St. Piran Collegiate Church.
Minster or Talkarn Priory.
Scilly Priory.
Tregony Priory.
Tywardreath Priory.
St. Anthony, Cell of Plympton.
St. Michael of Lammana Cell.
Truro Convent.
Endellion Collegiate Church.
Glasney Collegiate Church.
St. Michael's (Penkevil) Collegiate Church.
St. Teath Collegiate Church.
Helston Hospital of St. John the Baptist.
Liskeard Lazar-house.

Of the twenty-three religious houses enumerated the first nine are mentioned in Domesday Book, which also mentions the priests of St. Neot, the lands of St. Constantine and of St. Goran and the honour of St. Che (*Honor St. Chei*). There are also a few churches which call for examination like those of St. Kew, Mawnan and Manaccan whose religious character is omitted in both. Languihenoc and Gerrans have been already considered. It is obvious that to give a full and complete review of all of them would require not a chapter but a volume.

Before attempting to deal with the subject, within even the narrowest possible limits, we may profitably ask ourselves what courses were open to the members of monastic communities, which had been in the ascendant until the Saxon Conquest of Cornwall, in order that they might come into line with the new ecclesiastical régime? Three courses presented themselves. The first was to allow themselves to be disbanded as the regular clergy were compelled to be at the time of Henry's reformation; the second was to conform to the rules of one or other of the recognised western orders and to become affiliated to it; the third was to transform their convents of regular clergy into colleges or collegiate churches of secular clergy. No doubt there was a strong conservative party who resisted all change, otherwise it would be difficult to understand the spoliation of which there are traces during the Saxon period and of which after the Norman Conquest there is abundant proof in Domesday Book. Of the three courses which have been suggested the third seems to have been favoured under the Saxons and the second under the Normans.

Taking the nine monastic bodies which stand at the head of the foregoing list in order, it will suffice to say that after serving as the seat of an abbot-bishop the monastery of St. Petrock probably became collegiate and parochial. In Domesday Book it is always referred to as St. Petrock or the Church of St. Petrock. The date of its reconstruction as a monastery is obscure. There does not appear to be any evidence to show to which of the religious orders it belonged until the *Ordinatio* of the Priory by Bishop Grandisson in 1347, in which it is ordained that the prior and convent shall celebrate the Divine Office and observe vigil, fast, silence and prayer according to the rule of Blessed Augustine. Long before that date it had therefore doubtless become a convent of the Black Canons. Sir John Maclean expressly states, though on what authority I have not been able to discover, that it was Bishop William Warelwast (1107–1136) who settled therein regular canons of St. Augustine. In the *Taxatio* of the vicarage, by Bishop Bronescombe in 1269, the vicar was assigned, as a part of his emolument, the victuals (*liberacionem*) of one canon.

The monastery of St. Germans was served by secular canons before the Norman Conquest. Bishop Leofric (1046–1073) removed them and introduced canons regular. In 1270 Bishop Bronescombe ordered the excommunication of certain persons concerning whom he vouchsafes no particulars save that they were *Sathane satellites, proprie salutis immemores* and that they had expelled those whom he had sent to take charge of the priory during the vacancy caused by the death of Richard the late prior. His letter is valuable because it affords evidence that the bishop of Exeter claimed absolute power over the priory and its possessions so long as there was no prior appointed, and apparently the right of confirming the prior's appointment.

Of St. Michael's Mount some particulars will be found in Chapter X.

The church of St. Stephen by Launceston was like that of St. German served by secular canons at the time of the Domesday Survey. By Bishop William Warelwast (1107–1138) to whom Ralph the dean of St. Stephens had surrendered the deanery it was made an Augustinian priory and so remained until the dissolution of the religious houses by Henry VIII. Harassed and despoiled by Robert Count of Mortain in the years which followed the Norman Conquest, under the fostering care of Reginald Earl of Cornwall (1140–1175) and Richard King of the Romans (1225–1272), it soon became the wealthiest of the religious houses in Cornwall. The relations between the parochial church of St. Stephen and the priory are somewhat obscure. The church was taxed independently of the priory in 1291, but in the *Inquisitio nonarum* of 1346 the church was assessed at £10, of which 40s. was chargeable to the prior.

The collegiate church of St. Buryan is undoubtedly an early instance of the conversion of a Celtic monastery to a recognised English type. King Athelstan by charter gave a small piece of his land in a place which is called the church of St. Berrian . . . to be free of all taxation unless the clerks who had promised him their prayers, viz. 100 masses, 100 psalters and daily supplications failed, to perform their task. The place which is called the church of St. Berrian was evidently Eglosberria or Eglosveryan, of which we have already spoken. In later times it was advantageous to the dean and his fellows to cite Athelstan as their founder and their church as a royal chapel. All that the Saxon King did for them was probably to guarantee to them security of tenure for the lands which they already held and freedom from payment of geld.

The Canons of St. Crantock who held the manor of

Langorock at the time of the Survey (1086) also survived the various changes made in the constitution of their community until their dissolution in 1536. Robert, Count of Mortain, had already seized their lands when the Survey was made. His son, Count William, founded the Cluniac house at Montacute in Somerset, and to it he is said to have given the church of St. Crantock. It is certain that in 1236 the prior of Montacute transferred the church and its possessions to William Briwer, bishop of Exeter. The bishop thenceforth became patron of the deanery and prebends. In 1291 there were on the foundation a dean and nine prebendaries. St. Crantock had become a typical collegiate church. The several stages through which it passed leave no doubt that as Langorock it had established its claim to considerate treatment by Saxon and Norman alike.

Of St. Keverne we learn from Domesday Book that the canons of St. Achebran had one manor which was called Lannachebran, which the same saint had held in the Confessor's time. There is, however, evidence of its quasi-prebendal character more than a century before the Survey was made.[1] By Richard, Earl of Cornwall and King of the Romans, the church was given to the abbot and convent of Beaulieu for the good of his own soul and that of King John his father.[2] The vicarage was taxed by Bishop Bronescombe, in 1260, very unfavourably to the vicar, there being assigned to the abbot and convent of Beaulieu more than five-sixths of the income. Leland, writing about the year 1530, states that near "The Paroch church of S. Keveryn otherwise

[1] *Jour. Arch. Assocn.*, XXXIX, 282.

[2] Pat. Roll, 18 Edw. III, 1345.

Piranus," there is a sanctuary with ten or twelve dwelling houses and hard by "there was a sel of monkes but now gonn home to ther Hed Hows." These monks were doubtless Cistercians from Beaulieu who, for some reason or another, had been temporarily resident in the parish. The appropriation of the church by Earl Richard, and its taxation by Bishop Bronescombe, had left it a rather poorly endowed vicarage, of which the patronage and greater tithes belonged to Beaulieu. That Lannachebran was originally Celtic and monastic does not admit of doubt.

The account supplied by Domesday Book respecting St. Pieran (Perranzabuloe) is very illuminating. "The Canons of St. Pieran," so the statement runs, "have a manor called Lanpiran, which in the time of King Edward they held freely. . . . From this manor have been taken away two manors which in the time of King Edward rendered to the Canons of St. Pieran four weeks' farm (*firmam iii septimanarum*). Of these manors Berner holds one of the Count. And from the other hide which Odo holds of St. Pieran the Count has taken away all the stock (*pecuniam*). These two manors rendered to the Dean by way of custom 20s. in addition to the said farm (*firmam*)." The first of these two manors was that of Tregebri, which elsewhere in Domesday Book is described as being "of the honour[1] of St. Perann." The Count of Mortain took from both all that had

[1] Another honour is mentioned in the same record, viz. that of St. Cheus, which awaits identification. The Exeter book reads correctly that Tremar uustel is *de honore S. Chei*, whereas the Exchequer version has belongs *ad honore S. Chei*. This led General James to translate the words "belongs to the honours of Chei": *honore* is probably an abbreviation for *honorem* and the full stop after the *S* a contraction of *Sancti*.

formerly belonged to the saint. Dean and canons were swept away at an early date and the church given by Henry I to the dean and chapter of Exeter. When the vicarage was taxed in 1269, to the vicar was assigned the altarage of the mother church of St. Piran and of the chapel, together with all the offerings derived from the exposition of the relics, the vicar rendering a yearly tribute of six marks to the dean and chapter. The relics referred to were those of St. Piran the founder of the church, concerning which some interesting particulars are supplied in an inventory of the year 1281. Among other treasures mention is made of a reliquary in which is kept the head of St. Pyeran, with the rest of the relics secured with iron and a lock, a hearse in which the body of Pyeran is placed for processions, a tooth of St. Brendan and a tooth of St. Martin within a silver box, also a pastoral staff of St. Pyeran adorned with silver and gold and precious stones. Two centuries later when making St. Agnes parochial, the bishop ordained that if the parishioners of St. Pyran should bring the saint's relics to St. Agnes in procession as formerly, on Rogation Tuesday, they should receive honourable welcome and the oblations presented in the chapel of St. Agnes according to custom.

There has been much doubt concerning the identity of St. Piran. From the inventory of 1281 it would seem that at that time he was identified with St. Kieran of Saighir in Ireland, otherwise it would be difficult to account for the presence at Perranzabuloe of relics of St. Brendan, the friend to whom the saint sent a supply of milk in the form of a milch cow, and of those of St. Martin the founder of churches in Ossory, St. Kieran's native county, a person so highly esteemed by the saint that he extracted a promise from him that when they died they should be buried in the same grave. It is certain that in the thirteenth century, and a fortiori in the eleventh century, the foundation of St. Piran was regarded as Celtic and that the church claimed to have in its custody the crozier of its episcopal founder.

"The canons of St. Probus have one manor which is called Lanbrabois (Lamprobus. *Exch. D.*) which King Edward held at the time of his death." Such is the testimony of Domesday Book. The name of the manor suggests a monastic origin, but nothing whatever appears to be known of the saint or of the founder of the prebendal church. Had St. Edward been the founder it is probable that some use would have been made of the circumstance by succeeding generations. King John confirmed the grants of the church made by his ancestor (*avi*) Henry I and by his father Henry II to the bishop and cathedral church of Exeter.[1] By Bishop Briwer it was appropriated to the office of treasurer of the cathedral, together with the patronage of the five prebends, but the patronage was subsequently transferred to Bishop Bronescombe and exercised by him and his successors until the suppression of the prebends by Edward VI.

Having briefly considered the religious houses—using that term in its widest sense—concerning which mention is made in Domesday Book, it is worth while to pass on to those whose endowments either excited not the rapacity of the Norman, or were too slender to find a place in the Great Survey, and to those which were evidently founded after the Norman Conquest.

[1] *Monasticon*, p. 72.

Taking them in the order already indicated, we have the five establishments dignified by the name of priories.

The priory of St. Cyricus or St. Cyriacus in the parish of St. Veep is stated by Lysons to have been founded by William Count of Mortain, but no authority is quoted for the statement. In 1236 Bishop Briwer wishing to relieve the church of St. Nonn (probably the neighbouring church of Pelynt) from a yearly charge of six marks, four shillings and three pence heretofore payable to the little cell (*cellula*) of St. Cyricus, granted to the latter out of the revenues of his see a yearly payment of five marks. The cell was affiliated to the Cluniac priory of Montacute in the county of Somerset and was for a long time in the patronage of the family of that name. It is futile to speculate respecting its origin, and it is not safe to say that it was of Saxon or Norman origin, for St. Carreuc is found in three Breton parishes.[1]

The priory of Minster or Talkarn described as the church of St. Merthian of Laminster was, somewhere about the year 1130, given by William, son of Nicholas (Botreaux), to the monks of the Benedictine abbey of St. Sergius at Angers. Here again we have monastic associations suggested by the locality of the priory. Laminster was apparently already a place-name when the gift was made little more than half a century after the Norman Conquest. The priory, by reason of its connection with the French abbey, was suppressed during the fourteenth century.

The priory or cell of St. Nicholas, situated on the island of Tresco, Scilly, was probably Celtic in origin. The Charter of Henry I granting to the abbot and

[1] Loth, *Les Noms des Saints bretons*, p. 19.

church of Tavistock and to its monk Turold, the churches and land in Scilly uses the following words to limit and describe the tenure of the land—it is to be held " just as the monks or rather hermits (*monachi aut heremite melius*) held it in the time of King Edward of Burgald bishop of Cornwall."

Tavistock was a Benedictine abbey founded in the latter half of the tenth century. The rule of St. Benedict was broad and elastic, and monasteries could and did embrace it without parting entirely with their traditions.[1] It was, in fact, the only rule recognised in England during the whole of the Saxon period. Admitting all this the phrase "monks or rather hermits," is so studiously vague as to imply a doubt as to whether the brothers had in the Confessor's day submitted to any recognised rule whatever. It is certain that while bringing them into a closer relationship with Tavistock the King intended to enforce a stricter discipline, otherwise his further provision that they should, like "the King's own prebendaries" have his peace and protection, would have been unnecessary. The King does not confirm any supposed charter of Athelstan or of Edward, but gives the religious community at Scilly to the abbey at Tavistock, and, apart from the reference to the latter King, there is nothing to lead us to regard the monks as Benedictine or as affiliated to the abbey until Henry's charter was granted. As a cell of Tavistock, the Scilly monastery appears to have existed until the suppression of the mother house, but little is known of it subsequent to the middle of the fifteenth century.

Tregony Priory. At an early date the churches of

[1] Gasquet, *English Monastic Life*, p. 214.

St. James, Tregony, and of St. Cuby, appear to have accepted the rule of St. Augustine and to have been constituted a cell of the abbey of de Valle in Normandy. When and by whom this appropriation was made is unknown, but it is certain that it was made after the Norman Conquest. In the year 1278 Bishop Bronescombe gave his sanction to the transfer of the priory of Tregony to the priory of Merton in the county of Surrey. This was in furtherance of an arrangement between the prior of Merton and the abbot of de Valle, whereby the possessions of the former in the diocese of Bayeux were exchanged for those of the latter in England. Bishop Quivel confirmed the sanction of his predecessor in 1282, and until the dissolution of the religious houses the cell, which had become a vicarage, belonged to the monastery of Merton.

Of Tywardreath Priory little need be said here. At the time of the Domesday Survey, Tywardreath was one of the thirty manors in Cornwall which had been given by the Conqueror to Richard Fitz Turold. By Richard the priory was founded and affiliated to the great Benedictine abbey of SS. Sergius and Bacchus at Angers. The list of charters recording successive endowments is exceptionally complete, and for genealogical purposes the charters are of very great value, but they afford no suggestion of a pre-Norman foundation.

The cell of St. Anthony in Roseland represented a survival of an order of things of which we have little recorded evidence. In the thirteenth century it derived its main support from the church of St. Gerrans. In the *Taxatio* of Pope Nicholas IV the prior of St. Anthony is assessed at the same amount for his portion in the church of St. Gerrans as the rector himself. A little more than a century later, in the *Inquisitio nonarum*, St. Anthony is described as a chapel (*capella*) of St. Gerrans. Such information as we have points to a quasi-monastic establishment of St. Gerrans, followed by a parish church at Gerrans and a small monastery at St. Anthony. The latter was made, at an early date, dependent on the Augustinian priory of Plympton, and in the earlier half of the sixteenth century consisted of two canons.

The Cell of St. Michael of Lammana, situated in the parish of Talland opposite Looe Island, which formed a portion of its possessions, was given by John de Solenny in the twelfth century to the Benedictine abbey of Glastonbury. Richard, Earl of Cornwall, granted to the abbot a licence to farm out its revenues, and this probably accounts for the scant information supplied by the public records respecting the cell. The name Lammana points to Celtic monasticism.

The Convent of the Preaching Friars at Truro throws no light upon the subject before us. The friars first came to England in the year 1221. It is a striking proof of the rapidity with which the order spread that Bishop Bronescombe should have dedicated their church at Truro in 1259.

The origin of the Collegiate Church of Endellion is obscure. In 1273 the rectory belonged to the prior and convent of Bodmin; in 1342 Bodmin or King's prebend belonged to the same; in 1265 Marny's prebend belonged to the family of Bodrugan, and in 1266 Trehaverock prebend belonged to the family of Modret. The parish of Endellion was not in St.

Petrock's hundred of Pawton, nor do any of its three Domesday manors appear to have belonged to the saint. It would therefore seem as if the advowson or a moiety of it had been given to the priory after its reconstitution on English lines. In any case it would be rash to claim a pre-Norman origin for Endellion Collegiate Church.

The similar establishment at Glasney, near Penryn, owed its foundation to Bishop Bronescombe, who in 1267 consecrated the church of St. Thomas the Martyr and its churchyard. Glasney was an entirely new college, not the rehabilitation of an earlier institution, and on that account it does not enter into the present enquiry.[1]

The church of St. Michael Penkevil was made collegiate in 1319, as the result of the benefaction of Sir John de Trejagu. It was to be administered by an archpriest and three fellows who were to live under the same roof and to dine at the same table. It had no early monastic associations.

The date of the erection of St. Teath into a Collegiate Church is more obscure. Between the years 1258 and 1264 Bishop Bronescombe founded two prebends in St. Teath church, and, inasmuch as the number of prebends does not appear ever to have exceeded two, it is probable that the church owed its prebendal character solely to the bishop.

The Hospital of St. John the Baptist at Helston and the Lazar house at Liskeard, being comparatively modern foundations, need not be examined.

Reference has been made to three churches or religious houses—it is not clear which is the appro-

[1] Mr. Thurstan C. Peter has written an interesting and reliable account of *Glasney Collegiate Church* (Camborne, 1903).

priate term—which are mentioned in Domesday Book, but which are omitted in the *Monasticon.*

In the former document it is stated that St. Constantine has half a hide of land which in the time of King Edward was free of all service, but since the Count of Mortain received the land it has always rendered geld unjustly like villeins' land. This land, known as the manor of Tucoyes, was bestowed upon Wihumar and henceforth lost to the Church. The exemption from geld implies a monastic foundation, but no other trace of monastic origin has been found in connection with the church of St. Constantine.

Of St. Neot it is stated that the saint held a manor called Neotstou, consisting of two hides of land in the time of the Confessor, Godric being the priest in charge, and that the Count of Mortain has despoiled the priests of all their land save one (Cornish) acre. It is also stated that the two hides of land have never rendered geld. Monastic the church of St. Neot undoubtedly was, but in this case we have trustworthy historical evidence to prove that it was not Celtic but Saxon. St. Neot had himself founded the house in Saxonised territory. No trace of its original character is to be found in later documents. It would therefore seem that it had already become (in 1086) purely parochial.

The honour of St. Cheus or Che, of which the manor of Tremaruustel was a member at the time of the Domesday Survey, has hitherto resisted all attempts at identification. It probably represents a moribund and extinct monastic holding of considerable extent.

The Domesday manor of St. Mawnan (wrongly written Maiuian or Mawan in both copies) had fallen into the King's hand before the Conquest. But the church of St. Mawnan is referred to in many subsequent translations under the name of Minster, which suggests a monastic origin.

Manaccan, the monks' church, calls for no comment.

A very interesting and convincing example of the conversion of a purely Celtic monastic house to English uses is supplied by St. Kew. On linguistic grounds alone Professor Loth arrived at the conclusion that Docco, the monastery where St. Sampson made the acquaintance of St. Winniau, was St. Kew. An examination of the various forms under which the church is described in the Episcopal Registers revealed the forms Landoho, Lanho and Lanow. A Patent Roll of 1307 furnished the following statements, viz. that King Edgar (958–975) gave to the canons of Plympton two carucates of land, 100s. of rent in Landoho and the church there for the support of two canons celebrating divine service there and dispensing alms and hospitality to the poor, to pilgrims and other guests, that in a case tried before John de Berewyk and other justices (circa 1300) it was shown that the prior and convent of Plympton had failed to fulfil the above conditions and that, taking into account all the circumstances, the King now (1307) grants to the prior and convent the right to substitute a secular vicar and chaplain for the two canons at Landoho.

An examination of the Plympton charters showed that Henry I gave the church of Tohou to William Warelwast, bishop of Exeter, and that he gave the church to the priory of canons regular which he founded at Plympton in the year 1121. No one can doubt that Tohou and Docco are variants of the same word, which is found in Brittany as Tohou and Ohou. It is not difficult to follow the various acts of spoliation. King Edgar evidently reduced the patrimony of the Celtic monastery to the amount specified above while retaining the manor of Landoho, which until the Norman Conquest embraced the manors of Poundstock and St. Gennys. The three manors passed as an undivided whole to Earl Harold as demesne lands. By the Conqueror they were given to the Count of Mortain. Henry I claimed the remaining revenue of the monks and gave it to the bishop who transferred it to Plympton priory. Edgar's gift to Plympton was a legal fiction which enabled the priory to evade responsibilities which were implied in the charter of Henry I and explicitly stated in that of Henry II when canons regular were substituted for secular canons.[1]

In brief, St. Kew was the site of an important Celtic monastery which, visited by St. Sampson in the days of St. Winniau, despoiled by King Edgar and stripped bare by Henry I, nevertheless retained some semblance of its ancient glory until the latter half of the thirteenth century.

As the result of the above examination it will be observed that of the twenty-six religious houses about one-half afford evidence of Celtic origin. In some cases the evidence is convincing; in some it is of itself insufficient to convince. Taken as a whole, it adds considerably to the weight of the argument which is here advanced, namely, that in Cornwall the Celtic form of Christianity had not wholly disappeared at the time of the Norman Conquest. Of its secure and comprehensive hold upon the religious life of the

[1] *Monasticon*, p. 135.

whole county at an earlier period there is abundant proof in the names of the parishes. Excluding those which have been considered, fifteen bear the prefix *Lan*, the mark of monastic settlement. Others, like St. Erth (Lanudno), St. Madron (Landithy), St. Just-in-Penwith (Lafrowda), Kea (Landegy), Gulval (Lanisley), Lelant (Lananta), Lezant (Lansant), retained the prefix for a time, in an *alias*, which in some cases suggests an earlier dedication ; or, as in the case of Lanherne, Langunnet, Lanyhorne and Lanhadron still retain it in the name of the manor to which the advowson of the church was appendant ; while a very large number bear, without prefix or affix, the names of Celtic saints, many of them unknown to the outside world. From one end of the county to the other the impress of Celtic Christianity can be clearly traced. It is monastic in character. But it is not a monasticism which has intruded within the confines of parishes already formed, but a monasticism which has occupied the whole territory from the very first. This it is which, in the tenth and eleventh centuries, either finds itself gradually superseded by the newer parochialism, or which ensures, in some sort, its survival in collegiate bodies or in recognised monastic orders by submitting to new conditions and new ideas.

IX

CORNISH HERMITS

THE subject of English hermits and anchorites has been so exhaustively dealt with by Miss Rotha M. Clay[1] that a writer may well hesitate before he ventures to enter upon a small portion of the ground which she has covered. Miss Clay has performed her task with great judgment, learning and literary skill and with consummate diligence. So conscientiously and so impartially has she performed her task that the reader will seek in vain to discover whether she is in full sympathy with the hermit's vocation or the reverse. Her book will be read with pleasure and with profit by all.

The present writer wishes to acknowledge his obligations to Miss Clay, whose researches have both confirmed and supplemented conclusions already formed. The titles of the several chapters of her book are illuminating and suggestive, and the contents abundantly justify the distinction she has made between one type and another. We find ourselves introduced in succession to hermits of island and fen, forest and hillside, cave, lighthouse, highway and bridge, town, church and cloister.

Unless the student keeps in mind the fact that the eremitical impulse fulfilled itself in varied activities he will fail to understand its true nature and purpose.

[1] *Hermits and Anchorites of England,* Methuen & Co.

Here was no lawless spirit, disdaining the restraints of an ordered life, but "the fiery glow that whirls the spirit from itself away" to make it the ready instrument in God's hands for works of mercy, charity, counsel and service while seeking by prayer, meditation, vigil and fasting to attain unto perfection.

Again, while it is allowable to assume that the hermit who dwelt apart and in solitude was the precursor of the conventual body—the word monk implies as much—it nevertheless seems certain that, at the time when he first emerges into the clear light of Celtic history he is not, as popular fancy has imagined, a distraught enthusiast seeking refuge and rest from an evil and adulterous generation, but a tried soldier who has learnt in the convent by precept and by practice the art of war, and who goes forth in all the panoply of celestial might to fight singly and alone the enemies of his soul and to bring deliverance to others. No sooner has he achieved his own salvation than he sets about the salvation of his fellow-men. He has little in common with the self-regarding Christian of the *Pilgrim's Progress.* He is eager to be of use. He becomes a minister to the dwellers amid untrodden ways and in remote corners, it may be as a waywarden, a bridge repairer, or a light keeper, but in any case as the guide, the counsellor, the friend of all. Inevitably his sphere of influence widens out. Soon he has become equally necessary to the pilgrim, the traveller and to those who are round about him. As time goes on his cell and the little sanctuary where he and they have met for worship become hallowed by association, and, when he dies, a successor must be sought to carry on the tradition. The hermitage thus remains as a memorial of its founder long after his name has been forgotten.

Or, it may be, the hermit is joined by others like-minded and founds a religious community, a *lan* whose growth and permanence are promoted by the industry and self-denial of its members. This would seem to have been the normal course of events in Cornwall. In this case the individual founder is often content to leave his work to be carried on by others during his lifetime. He may be a bishop, priest, deacon or layman who determines to undergo the hardships of the wilderness for a season, but who has no intention of devoting his whole life to solitude. Diversities of gifts under the spell of a common impulse give rise to diversities of ministration and of operation.

Of the hermits of the Celtic period in Cornwall we have very little historical evidence. Presumptive evidence we have which, if it told against the traditional interpretation of early Christianity, would doubtless be held to possess great value. For example, we have, in the lives of the saints, references to ecclesiastical types and economic conditions which had been obsolete for centuries when some of those lives are held to have assumed their present literary form.

We have holy wells bearing the names of saints which are not the names of the patron saints of the parishes in which the wells are situated. We have legends which, for the purpose of comparative mythology, are highly esteemed. There are, for example, holy wells at St. Ingunger, Chapel Uny (St. Uny's) and Jetwells, but these are not the patrons of the parishes, though they are all three well-known Celtic saints. On the other hand, there are wells bearing the names of St. Levan, St. Madron, St. Clether, St. Keyne and St. Just (Venton—east) situated in the parishes which do bear their names. If the ancient Cornish churches derived their names from their founders or founders' kin it seems probable that the holy wells acquired their names from association with the saints whose names they bear.

There would be the same inducement for a hermit to fix his abode near a spring of water as there is for an Australian squatter to choose a similar spot for the headquarters of his sheep or cattle station. So late as A.D. 1086, when Domesday Book was compiled, the county of Cornwall was very sparsely populated. In the place-names may be recognised traces of a fauna long extinct but nevertheless extant in Celtic times.[1] It is necessary to bear in mind the transformation of the county, which during the last thirteen centuries has resulted from increased settlement and the more extensive cultivation of land, in order to be in a position to estimate the value of the evidence supplied by the hagiographer.

Early in the sixth century St. Petrock succeeded St. Guron at Bodmin ; such is the tradition. Leland (circa 1540) thus records the event,[2] *Bosmana, id est, mansio monachorum in valle, ubi St. Guronus solitarie degens in parvo tugurio, quod reliquen(s) tradidit St. Petroco.* Guron was doubtless a hermit. Petrock enlarged the hermitage, which was situated in the valley where the town now stands and near the well which still bears the hermit's name, so as to make it

[1] Nancherrow and Carnyorth, two neighbouring hamlets in St. Just-in-Penwith, denote respectively the *valley of the stag* and *the hill of the roebuck*.

[2] Leland, *Collectanea*, i, 75.

capable of sheltering himself and three brethren. Guron is probably the same as Goran, the name-saint of the parish in the ancient deanery of Powder. Traces of the name are to be found in Brittany.[1]

William of Worcester (1478) introduces us to three Cornish hermits, Vylloc or Willow, Mybbard and Mancus. They were companions.

The first is described as a hermit and martyr born in Ireland and beheaded by Melyn's kinsfolk (*Melyn ys kynrede*) near the place (in Lanteglos-by-Fowey) where Walter, bishop of Norwich, was born.

From this place to the bridge of St. Willow, a distance of half a mile, he carried his (head) to a spot where the said church was built in his honour.[2] Mybbard, otherwise Calrogus, is stated to have been a hermit, the son of a King of Ireland, and his body is said to rest within the shrine (*scrinio*) of Cardynham Church. Mancus, their companion and a hermit, is said, on the authority of Robert Bracey, to lie in the church of Lanreath, within two miles of Fowey, and, on the authority of the canons of Launceston, in the parish of Lanteglos presumably at Bodinnick. All three are said to be commemorated on the same day, viz. the Thursday next before Whitsunday. William of Worcester's account of the three hermits is prefaced by the sentence " there were three brothers under the name of St. Genesius and each carried his head, one of them archbishop of Lismore." Is it possible that St. Gennys may be a corruption of a Latinised Greek word *συγγενεις* (kinsmen)? It is curious, in any case, that the feast of Cardynham and St. Gennys should be held on Whitsunday, that of

[1] Loth, *Les Noms des Saints bretons*, p. 48.

[2] *Parochial History of Cornwall*, Supplement, pp. 102, 110.

Lanteglos having been abandoned and that of Lanreath, whose patron is now given as Marnarch, being kept on the third of August. Anciently there was a chapel at Bodinnick bearing the name of St. John the Baptist. St. Willow is regarded as the patron of Lanteglos and Mybbard as the patron of Cardynham. When all due allowance has been made for accretions and errors in transmission it seems impossible to doubt that three Irish hermits were martyred at or near Lanteglos and commemorated by churches built in their honour.

St. Neot represents a prevalent type of religious which, from the first days of British Christianity until the eleventh century, combined the habits and aspirations of the hermit with the practical usefulness of the missionary. Neot was born in the earlier years of the ninth century of parents who were nearly related in blood to the West-Saxon Kings. Forsaking a military career for which he had been intended, he entered the monastery of Glastonbury, where he received Holy Orders and became eminent for piety, learning, wisdom and counsel. The fear of popular applause drove him forth into the wilderness. He fixed his abode in the Cornish parish which now bears his name, near to a hamlet then known as Hamstoke and therefore apparently already a Saxon settlement. Here he lived seven years. At the end of that time he visited Rome and was advised by the Holy Father to renounce his habit of solitary devotion to return home and scatter the word of God among the people of Cornwall.

He came back to Hamstoke and founded there the college of priests of which mention is made in Domesday Book. At Hamstoke he was visited more than once by his kinsman Alfred the Great, who hunted in the neighbourhood and who is said to have been healed at the shrine of St. Guerir of a malady which had afflicted him from boyhood.

St. Neot's hermitage was near the spring which is about half a mile west of the church and is known as St. Neot's well. In his day there appear to have been two pools, one of them with an unique unfailing supply of three fishes, of which one only was to be caught in a day, and the other, a pool in which the saint was wont to stand daily while repeating the Psalter. Many stories are told of the saint's sojourn by the well. The fox which stole his shoe, the rescue of the doe from the hounds, the theft of his working bullocks and the employment of stags for the ploughing of his land are sufficiently well known.

By the advice of St. Neot King Alfred is said to have restored the English school at Rome. The saint continued to be abbot of his own foundation until his death, which took place on the 31st of July, 877. He was buried in the church which he had built on the site of the chapel of St. Guerir. About a century later his bones were fraudulently removed to the monastery of Eynesbury in Huntingdonshire.

There are several points of interest. There does not appear to have been any marked difference between St. Neot's eremitical career and that of others of Cornish origin. This may be owing to the late composition of the lives of many of the saints. The substitution of St. Neot for St. Guerir as the name-saint of the church has many precedents and would call for no remark here did it not afford a good example of what was also in Cornwall a fairly general practice, of which the proofs are not abundant—that of calling churches after the names of their founders.[1]

At this point it is convenient to call attention to the story of *Tristan and Iseult,* which has been shown to be of Cornish origin and which assumed literary form probably towards the end of the eleventh century. Most of the places mentioned in the story are found in Cornwall and, although the actors in the drama are presumed to have lived some five centuries before their deeds were committed to writing, there are nevertheless inferences to be derived from the record of them which have a direct bearing upon our subject even if we suppose the setting of the story to have been, at the time, comparatively modern. The following episode is an example. During the sojourn of Tristan and Iseult in the forest of Morrois (Moreske), which then extended from the Fal to the Helford river, they meet with a hermit, Ogrin by name, who does not hesitate to give them some much-needed advice. He calls them to repentance and then listens patiently to Tristan's excuses. It is not suggested that in admonishing them he is exceeding his duty. He is described as a hermit with a hermitage in the forest, a personage quite distinct from the parish priest, whose sphere of influence had already become a recognised geographical unit, as is shown by the following passage :

> En Cornoualle n'a parroise
> Ou la novele n'en angoise
> Que, qui porroit Tristan trover
> Qu'il en feïst le cri lever.

Ogrin, as a man of sense, advises the Queen to return

[1] The name of Neot's predecessor, like that of Veronica, may have been suggested to Asser by the reputed miracle ; but, if so, it would not invalidate the truth of the narrative so far as it relates to the successive founders of the church.

home, and himself undertakes the delicate task of reconciling the lovers to King Mark.

Throughout the narrative he is represented as a man of God. It does not seem to have occurred to the romancer that there is something slightly incongruous in selecting a hermit for a shopping expedition to the market of St. Michael's Mount, where, for the fair Iseult :

> Assés achate ver et gris
> Dras de soie et de porpre bis,
> Escarlates et blanc chainsil,
> Asez plus blanc que flor de lil,
> Et palefroi souef amblant
> Bien atorné d'or flanboiant.

The hermit, as a man of affairs, may have been familiar to those for whose ears the romance was intended. It is difficult, otherwise, to assign a reason why the writer exaggerated his character beyond the bounds of recognition. The position which the hermit occupied in the popular estimation, august as it undoubtedly was, was not more exalted than that which was voluntarily conceded to him by those who were highly placed. To this fact must doubtless be attributed the more or less successful attempts to perpetuate the office when its occupant was removed by death. It is therefore possible that in the hermit of Colemanshegg, mentioned in a Roll of 1258, we have a reference to one of Ogrin's successors.[1] Of this latter personage we know nothing save that Richard hermit of Colemanshegg received 50s. yearly to find a chaplain to celebrate divine service for the soul of Catherine the King's daughter.

But for this mention of Richard of Colemanshegg

[1] Colemanshegg is probably Kelmonseg (1308)=Kilmonseg (1332)=Kilmonsek (1427)=Kyllymansak (1442)=Calamansack (hodie), in Constantine parish, which in the eleventh century was embraced in the forest of Morrois.

the earliest notice of a Cornish hermit after the Norman Conquest would have been that contained in the Assize Roll of the 30th year of Edward I (1301–1302) in which it is recorded that *Thomas de Penmargh noctanter intravit domum Andreae Paugan heremitae infra capellam Divi Justi et eum occidit. Johannes filius Andreae heremitae primus invenitor.* The entry is under the heading of the hundred of Penwith. Penmargh is doubtless Penmarth in Wendron. Pagan, of which Paugan may be a variant, is not uncommon as a personal name in early records. We are not told why Thomas of Penmargh killed Andrew, or how long it was before John discovered the dead body of his father, but it looks as if Andrew had been seen alive the day before his death and found dead by his son the day after. Where was the hermitage ? It is described as below the chapel of St. Just, but St. Just was not a chapel (*capella*). It was a church (*ecclesia*), and the terms are never used indiscriminately. If it be allowable to render the passage " below a chapel of St. Just," that is, below a chapel in the parish of St. Just, the record is very significant.

For one of the most interesting spots in that parish is Chapel Carn Brea, upon the summit of which stood until 1816 a chapel of which a sketch was made by Dr. Borlase, who described it as being approached from the south side by a large flight of steps and as being twenty feet in height, and the roof arched with stone well wrought. Hals tells us it was about ten feet wide and fourteen feet long, with a window in the east end. Both writers speak of an immense heap of stones lying around it, suggesting a large vault or hermitage underneath. The chapel was pulled down in 1816 to build a barn elsewhere. When, in 1879, Mr. W. C. Borlase made an examination of the confused mass of stones which remained, and still remain, he failed to discover any trace of a hermit's cell, and concluded that the greater portion of the debris had done service as a covering for the prehistoric chambered grave which was found at a lower level. While it is not unlikely that the tumulus suggested, at a very early period, the site for the chapel to the first Christian solitary who found his way to that remote spot, the amount of stone there at the present time is too great to warrant the conclusion, unless the tumulus was of a type and size which has no rival in the county.

Some building doubtless existed besides the chapel, the size of which was obviously too small for public worship.

The most striking feature of Chapel Carn Brea is the commanding view which it affords not only of the Channel but of the whole of Penwith and of a large portion of the Lizard. No better spot could be chosen for a beacon.

Within a couple of hundred yards is the ancient mule track from Marazion to the Land's End. After reading Miss Clay's chapter on hermits as light-keepers, it seems impossible to doubt that the hermit of Chapel Carn Brea was one of those who in the day of small things performed that function, and whose simple signal was to the seafarer no less than to the traveller over the lonely moor a bright beacon of God. Andrew Paugan was probably only one of a long line of hermits who dwelt on the hill. A curious extract is found in Dr. Borlase's collections which, as one of the latest specimens of Cornish literature, has a value all its own and, as the witness of a tradition extant in the latter half of the seventeenth century, is useful for the present purpose. I am indebted to Mr. Henry Jenner for a transcript and translation of it.

"The Accusation of the Hermit (who liv'd in Chapel Karn Bray in Buryan) address'd to ye Duchess.

Rag an Arlothus woolaes Kernow
Dreth 'guz kibmias beniggas.

Why ra cavas dre eu an gwas Harry ma Poddrack broas.

Kensa, wit a hagar-awal iggeva gweel do derevoll war ren ny Keniffer termen dre ra ny moas durt Pedden an woolaes do Sillan. Nessa, wit an skavoll Crack-an-codna iggava setha war en cres a'n awles ewhall (cries tutton Harry an Lader) heb drog veeth. Tregga, wit an gurroll iggeva gwell gen askern skooth Davas, etc."

To the Countess of the Dominion of Cornwall.
By your sacred leave.

You shall find by him that this fellow Harry is a great witch.

First, from the stormy weather he does work to raise upon us every time that we do go from the end of the Land to Silly. Second, from the break-neck stool which he can (or does) sit upon in the middle of the high cliff (call'd The Chair of Harry the Thief), without any hurt. Thirdly, from a ship he does make with the bone of a shoulder of mutton.

Mr. Jenner is inclined to think that the "seat of Harry the thief" (Tutton Harry an Lader) refers to a piece of cliff at Tol Pedn Penwith called "Chair Ladder." The whole passage as it stands detached from the context (which has been lost) is little more than so much gibberish. Possibly it may have been so intended, for the romance, of which it is a fragment, was written by Mr. Boson for his children. But this consideration, assuming it to be well founded, would not rob the allusions of their evidential value. Quite the contrary. Every romance requires some element of fact or vraisemblance to recommend it to the popular imagination. Not more than half a mile from Chapel Carn Brea, at the foot of the hill, is Crows-an-Wra, the Witch's Cross, which may have suggested the character personified by Harry the Wizard of the break-neck stool. Some vague memories of the hermit who served the little chapel, tended the beacon and directed the travellers across the desolate moor doubtless still survived. Andrew Paugan was only one of the occupants of the cell, one who like many others in various parts of England spent his life in solitude, enduring privation and hardship and cultivating piety by prayer, meditation and active philanthropy. He was probably a widower when he gave himself to the career which Thomas of Penmargh, in the stillness of night, for some unknown reason brought to an untimely end.

The next mention of Cornish hermits is found in the *Inquisitio post-mortem* of Edmund, Earl of Cornwall.[1] Following the inventory of honours, lands and services held by him at the time of his death there is a list of the charges upon his estates and among them the entry: "alms to St. Philip of Restormel, hermit, and St. Robert of Penlyn, hermit." The earldom and its possessions reverted to the King on Earl Edmund's death, and we are therefore not surprised

[1] Inq. p.m., 28 Edw. I, 44 (4).

to find an entry in the Close Roll of the following year, 1301, which reads as follows : " To the sheriff of Cornwall. Order to deliver to brother Robert of Penlyn, hermit, the island surrounded (*inclusam*) by the water of Fawe with a rent of 56s. 2d. from certain tenants of the manor of Penkneth, to be held by him for life as he held them before the death of Edmund, Earl of Cornwall, by reason of whose death the sheriff took them into the King's hands ; on the same terms as the earl granted them, together with the houses built on the island, to Robert by his charter which the King has inspected."[1]

All attempts to identify the island have hitherto failed. The manors of Penlyn or Pelyn and Penkneth or Pennight are in the parish of Lanlivery, of which the river Fowey is, roughly speaking, the eastern boundary, but no island is now to be discovered in its course. The site of the hermitage of Restormel is also uncertain. It may have been that of the chapel of the Holy Trinity in the park, sometimes called the King's free chapel, to which frequent reference is made in the Rolls, and from which, according to an inventory made in 1338, a bell weighing 100 lbs. had been removed to the chapel within the castle walls of Restormel. There is nothing to lead us to suppose that St. Philip and St. Robert had successors. It is not improbable that royal chaplains were substituted for them.

In 1339 the Patent Roll records the King's protection granted to Roger Godman, hermit of the chapel of St. Mary by Liskeard (Liskerith), collecting about the realm the alms whereon he depends for subsistence.[2] It is probable that the chapel of St.

[1] *Calendar of Close Rolls*, 20 May, 1301, p. 488.

[2] Pat. R., 13 Edw. III, 1339.

Mary was the same as the King's free chapel of St. Mary in the park of Liskeard to which Edward II appointed Roger de Aqua his chaplain in 1316.[1] It must be distinguished from that of the Hospital of St. Mary Magdalen. The former appears to have become a chantry, for, in 1378, a royal grant was made to Richard Lagge, chaplain, that he might celebrate service in it, and in the same year the bishop issued a licence to him in which it is stated that he is to celebrate for the welfare of the King.[2] The chantry was suppressed by Edward VI, and the "Chapel of our Laydye" granted to Thomas Pomray in 1549.[3] It is interesting to compare the fortunes of this chapel with that of the Holy Trinity in the park of Restormel. Both of them appear to have been served originally by hermits, to have been converted into royal chapels and to have shared the same fate.

A little more than half a century later, in 1403, the following entry occurs in Bishop Stafford's register: "One Cecilia Moys, desiring to lead the contemplative life of an anchorite[4] in a certain house in the cemetery of Marhamchurch, the bishop on the 4th of May, 1403, commissioned Philip, abbot of Hartland, and Walter Dollebeare, vicar of Southill,

[1] *Ibid.*, 9 Edw. II, 1316.

[2] *Ibid.*, 1 Rich. II, 1378, and *Reg. Brantyngham*, p. 387.

[3] Pat. R., 3 Edw. VI, 1549.

[4] Hermit (Gr. Eremites, L. Heremita), one who lives in the desert; Anchorite (Gr. Anachoretes, L. Anchorita), one withdrawn from the world; Monk (Gr. Monachos, L. Monachus), one who dwells alone. The difference between a hermit and an anchorite was that the former was free to move from place to place, the latter was confined. The monk who had at first been a solitary soon became a member of an ordered and celibate community.

It is curious to notice that the impulse which created the hermit produced the monastery, and that, at a later date, the monastery incidentally produced the hermit.

to place her there under proper protection, assigning her till Christmas as a time of probation."

Churchyards were regarded as places specially suitable for the dwellings of anchorites as being dead to the world. It was, moreover, an obvious advantage to the parish priest that they should be near the church for the purpose of Communion. A second entry in the same bishop's register probably refers to the same anchorite, though the name is given as that of Lucy Moys, anchorite of Marhamchurch.

She receives on the 10th of October, 1405, a licence to choose her confessor. Another entry in the same register records a bequest of 40s. by Richard Tyttesburry, canon of Exeter, to the anchorite of Marhamchurch. His will was made on the 24th of February, 1405, and proved on the 7th of June, 1409.[1]

At St. Teath there was a hermit, name unknown, who in 1408, under the will of Sir William Bonevylle, received 20s. to pray for the soul of the testator: "al heremyte de Stetth pour prier pour moy." In the Lambeth manuscript the bequest is recorded "a lermytage de Stath," suggesting, but by no means proving, a permanent hermitage in the parish.[2]

Seven years later, in 1415: "Margaret an anchorite dwelling near Bodmin, having asked permission to migrate to the monastery of St. Bridget by Schene and to join the order settled there, is licensed by the bishop accordingly." To her or to her predecessor Richard Tyttesburry, whose name has been already mentioned, bequeathed in 1405 the sum of 40s.[3]

It has been generally supposed that Roche Rock, a natural and rugged monolith some 300 feet in

[1] *Register Stafford*, pp. 25, 251, 294.
[2] *Ibid.*, p. 391.
[3] *Ibid.*, pp. 25, 294.

height, situated in the parish which bears its name, was formerly the seat of a hermitage, and there is much to favour the supposition. Norden (1584) describes it as " a verie high, steepe and craggie rock, upon the top whereof is placed a cell or hermitage, the walls whereof are partly wroughte, and that with great labour out of the obdurate rock." In the illustration, which he gives, the building is complete with roof, windows and door. A detailed account is supplied by Davies Gilbert (1838), from which it appears that in his day the roof and upper chamber (as shown in Norden's plate) had already disappeared, the beam holes of the chamber being the only evidence that such a chamber had existed. The dimensions of what is supposed to have been the chapel are given by him : the length 20 feet, the breadth 12 feet and the height 10 feet.

There are apparently only two purposes for which a building, at such an elevation and in so desolate and remote a spot, could serve—that of a beacon house or of a hermitage. The former is the less probable explanation because of more suitable sites in the neighbourhood. The lack of documentary evidence in support of the latter hypothesis is not surprising and will carry little weight with those who reflect that it is only, as it were, by accident that we have any evidence at all respecting the other hermitages in the county. Comparing the cell on Roche Rock with other similar cells in various parts of England it may be inferred that the building was at one and the same time used by its occupants for both purposes.

The foregoing survey discloses no such secrets as might have been expected. It leaves the story of

Cornwall's conversion where we found it. The key of the position remains undiscovered—the key wherewith to open and unroll the unwritten record of the struggles of those first fateful days when the Christian faith gained a foothold in the land. We are thrown back upon the witness of an age so late as to render the witness of doubtful value. If we refer to it, it is with diffidence, having little or no hope that, as evidence, it will receive the consideration it deserves. Yet in spite of all that may be urged against any particular legend, we must not forget that hagiographer and monk, chronicler and poet, cross and cell, holy well and church, all proclaim the same story and tell the same tale when they represent the heralds of the good tidings as wandering in deserts and in mountains and in dens and caves of the earth. The account of St. Sampson's visit and the legend of St. Petrock are but types of the rest.

It would doubtless help towards the solution of the problem if something more definite could be known of the quarter whence the earliest of those heralds came. Was it from Gaul, from Lerins, from the East or from Rome ? We know that St. Hilary of Poitiers, in the middle of the fourth century, dedicated his treatise *De Synodis* to the bishops of the British provinces, that St. German of Auxerre accompanied by St. Lupus of Troyes came over to Britain in 429 to assist in extirpating the Pelagian heresy. Does this point to some closer and deeper connection than that of mere propinquity between the Churches of Gaul and of Britain ?

The intercourse between Rome and Britain, the Roman soldiers and merchants who during the occupation were brought into daily contact with the Britons could not fail to effect some change in the religious attitude of the latter. It is not, however, this slow, silent, indirect influence which excites our interest. It is rather of that direct attack upon paganism which so far succeeded as to impress a definite character and to make it possible to speak of Celtic Christianity as a distinct type that we wish to hear.

We allow that the same truths when accepted by different races produce different effects and find expression in different ways. An orthodox Russian Churchman and an English Churchman profess the same creeds, accept the same Scriptures, and are in all essentials of one heart and of one soul; yet it will be some time before the latter can be got to feel at home in the public worship of the former. Race, temperament and tradition reveal themselves in external modes of worship. This is true, but it is not sufficient to account for the rôle of isolation assumed by the British Church and by the daughter Church of Brittany. Some external influence appears to have been at work at a very early period, monastic in character, which was unfavourable to the cultivation of close relations with the rest of Western Christianity. It could hardly have been either of Roman or of Gaulish origin. Had it been Roman it would have constituted a bond of union instead of being, as it was, a barrier against which Augustine could not prevail; had it been Gaulish it would probably have been attempered by intercourse with the source of its inspiration. Possibly it came from the Mediterranean or from the East by way of Marseilles.

X

ST. MICHAEL'S MOUNT

IT is of little consequence to consider when and by whom the suggestion was first put forward, but it was one which captivated all who were anxious to endow their native county with a unique distinction. The suggestion was that St. Michael's Mount was identical with the island of Ictis, mentioned by Diodorus Siculus about the beginning of the first century before the Christian era.

Assuming the truth of this hypothesis, for which, indeed, many cogent arguments could be urged, historical writers were enabled to make a better start in the case of Cornwall than in the case of any other English county.

It is therefore somewhat disquieting to find a distinguished geologist staking a great reputation upon a counter-theory which, though promulged so recently as the year 1905, has at the present moment the support of the majority of those who are competent to form a judgment of its scientific value. Mr. Clement Reid, F.R.S., basing his arguments upon the evidence of geology and physical geography, has been able to show[1] that, nineteen hundred years ago, the Isle of Wight was, at high water, an island and, at low water, a peninsula answering exactly to the description of the island of Ictis given by Diodorus,

[1] Archæologia, LIX (2), 281 *et seq.*

whereas St. Michael's Mount was at that time "an isolated rock rising out of a swampy wood." On the other hand, however, it is only fair to say that Prof. Oman, who has doubtless examined and weighed, with his accustomed acumen, Mr. Reid's reasoning and conclusions, remains unconvinced. The Rev. H. R. Coulthard has broached a new theory, which has perhaps not yet received the attention it deserves ; it is that Ictis was the entire peninsula of Western Penwith. As against this, there is the evidence of Pliny who, on the authority of Timæus, states that the island of Mictis, apparently only another form of Ictis, was distant six days' sail along the British coast, a statement which is as fatal to the claims of Penwith as to those of the Mount itself.

The question can hardly be said to be finally decided, but the prevailing opinion is in favour of the Isle of Wight.

The Mount has had several names. In the life of St. Cadoc[1] it is called Dinsul, which probably means the citadel of the sun.

St. Cadoc is said to have visited his aunt St. Keyne there, and to have miraculously provided the Mount with a supply of water.

By the Cornish it was called Careg Cowse, or Karrek-luz-en-Kuz, which William of Worcester correctly translates "Hoar Rock in the Wood." It would be interesting to discover earlier evidence of this name. Its survival in the fifteenth century[2]—in spite of the monastic and military occupation of the Mount for many centuries—is very remarkable and seems to

[1] Cott. MS. Vesp. A. XIV.

[2] The name survived until the Cornish language was obsolete. Boson (1702) uses it.

carry us back to the time when Mr. Reid's description was exactly realised.

At some period, very difficult to determine, the Mount became known as Mons Tumba.[1] A charter in the Otterton custumal recording the reconstitution of St. Michael's priory, in the reigns of Henry I, and Stephen, enjoins that the Cornish monks shall receive the blessing of their abbot at Monte Tumba unless, perchance, it shall please him to come into Cornwall and bless them there; from which it may be inferred that the religious house in Monte Tumba was at that time identified with Mont St. Michel in Normandy, although the latter was then, at an earlier date and long afterwards, commonly described as St. Michael in Periculo Maris.[2] When dealing with the medley of notes collected by William of Worcester it will be necessary to bear this in mind.

The Mount was associated with St. Michael before the Norman Conquest, in all probability before the Saxon invasion of Cornwall.

As Professor Loth has pointed out,[3] the name-saints (*hagio-onomastique*) of ancient Brittany are entirely national. "With the exceptions of some apostles, of St. Michael, St. Matthew, of St. Peter who has given his name to Ploubezre, it is useless to seek for them in Gaul and the Roman Church: they

[1] See dispensation granted by Thomas (Cranmer) to John Arscott, archpriest of St. Michael *de Monte Tumba Exoniensis diocesis* (*Monasticon*, p. 30).

[2] The statue of the Blessed Virgin in the parish church of Mont St. Michel, known as the black virgin, also bears the name of Notre Dame de Mont Tombe and the small island in the bay about two miles from Mont St. Michel is called Tombelaine. Tumba (*twmp* in Welsh from Latin *tumulus*) and Tombelaine (the Teutonic diminutive of Tumba) are probably derived from the prehistoric remains of which there is now no trace.

[3] *Les Noms des Saints bretons*, p. 5.

are all of them insular (British or Irish) or native Breton." The same may be said of Cornwall with very few exceptions. The position assigned to St. Michael was everywhere unique. At some time subsequent to the Babylonish captivity St. Michael came to be had in special veneration of the Jews. From apostolic times in the East and from the fifth century, at least, in the West, he was received into the devotional system of the Christian Church. Nothing could have been more sane or scriptural than the honour paid to St. Michael. As the Prince of God's people and the Captain of the heavenly hosts[1] (*militiae celestis signifer*) he, who had prevailed against the Spirit of evil, might well be expected to lend his aid when the wrestling was against the spiritual hosts of wickedness in heavenly places. And what spot so worthy to be the site of an earthly fane for one whose warring is in the regions above man's head, as the lonely mountain's top. There is a sense of security felt by those who live on, or surrounded by, hills even now when so many ages have run since they were remotely responsible for it. The proper seat of the Archangel was clearly on the hill-top. They "found him an house" accordingly on the Cornish Mount, on Rowtor, on Rame Head, on Penkevil, on Caerhayes and on the western Carn Brea. Whether the cult of St. Michael superseded some earlier pagan cult in Cornwall it is impossible to say. Until some evidence is forthcoming it can serve no useful purpose to dilate upon the possible identity of Michael, Elias and Helios, or upon the possibility of one whose most notable achievement was the destruction of sun worship on Mount

[1] Dan. x. 13, 21; xii. 1; Rev. xii. 7.

Carmel, being himself its personification to after ages.

That there was a religious community at the Mount bearing the name of St. Michael before the Norman Conquest hardly admits of doubt. All the saints, with three exceptions, found there by William of Worcester, in the Calendar, were Celtic and insular.

The late Professor Freeman and Mr. Horace Round have, however, expressed a contrary opinion based upon the doubtful authenticity of two charters, certain particulars of which, connected chiefly with their attestation, are admittedly and obviously inaccurate.

The first of these charters[1] purports to be a grant made by Edward the Confessor, "King of the English, to Michael the Archangel for the use of the brethren serving God in that place, of St. Michael near the Sea, of the whole of the lands of Vennefire and of the port called Ruminella with its mills and fisheries." This charter bears the signatures of Edward the King, Robert archbishop of Rouen, Herbert bishop of Lisieux, Robert bishop of Coutances, Ralph, Vinfred, Nigell the sheriff, Anschitill, Choschet and Turstin. The second charter[2] claims to be a grant by Robert Count of Mortain to the monks of St. Michael in Periculo Maris (Normandy), of St. Michael's Mount in Cornwall with half a hide of land and a market on Thursdays; and three (Cornish) acres of land in Amaneth, namely Trevelaboth, Lismanoch, Trequaners and Carmailoc, the signatories being King William (the Conqueror), Queen Matilda, Count Robert, William Rufus the King's son, Henry the Boy (prince), Robert Count of Mortain, Matilda (his) countess, their son William, William Fitz

[1] See appendix, p. 172. [2] *Ibid.*, p. 173.

Osborn, Roger de Montgomery, Tossetin the sheriff, Warin and Turulf.

To the grant there are added, 1—a confirmation of it by Livric (Leofric), bishop of Exeter, bearing date 1085 ; and 2—a postscript signed by the bishop, exempting by command of Pope Gregory, the church of St. Michael in Cornwall from episcopal control and conveying a remission of one-third of their penance to those who should enrich, endow or visit the said church.

With regard to Edward's charter, it has been pointed out by more than one writer that Edward probably did not assume the title of King of the English until after the death of Hardicanute in 1042, and that Robert, archbishop of Rouen, died in 1037. It is not stated whence Dugdale obtained his copy of the charter, but a footnote by Oliver informs us that the MSS. of the *abbey* of St. Michael are preserved in the public library at Avranches ; and it is noteworthy that the charter in his *Monasticon* is labelled Carta Edwardi regis Anglorum pro *abbatia* Sancti Michaelis, and that the three episcopal signatories are *Norman* ecclesiastics. It is therefore possible that during his sojourn in Normandy Edward who :

> . . . loved the holy company
> Of people of religion,
> Who loved only all that was good ;
> Especially a monk who led
> A high and heavenly life

may have been induced to promise or to give Cornish lands to the Norman St. Michael and that his friends may have styled him Rex Anglorum, knowing that only when he became de facto King of the English could any benefit accrue to the abbey. But it seems more probable that a gift of lands was made by him to the Cornish St. Michael after Hardicanute's death and that after the Norman Conquest when the two religious houses were united by the cession of the Cornish priory to the Norman abbey the deed which may have borne the signature of Robert, archbishop of Canterbury, was altered so as to bear that of Robert, archbishop of Rouen. In that case the grant would have been made between 1050 and 1066. There were undoubtedly bold and fruitless attempts made on the part of the Norman abbots to enrich the Norman at the expense of the Cornish house, just as at a later period there were bold and successful attempts made to enrich the latter by borrowing the legends and traditions of the former.

The substantial genuineness of Edward's charter will be regarded as probable when it is remembered that no ultimate advantage can be shown to have accrued from it to either house. A spurious document would hardly have been preserved in the face of facts witnessing to its failure. Neither Domesday Book nor the *Inquisitio Geldi* makes mention of any possessions in Meneage belonging to St. Michael.

The suggestion offered in Chapter VI, viz. that the Meneage was at an early period monks' land both in name and in fact, may possibly account for the entire series of transactions. Grants to religious houses and for religious purposes have not infrequently been a trifling recompense made to Paul for the spoiling of Peter. It was notably so in the reign of King Henry VIII. If in the early part of the eleventh century the Meneage represented alienated, that is, usurped monastic land, no one would have been more disposed than King Edward to make restoration or to honour St. Michael by granting it to the Mount. It is not unlikely that the grant remained inoperative owing to the difficulty of making terms with the layfolk in possession.

In the appendix[1] to volume iv. of his *Norman Conquest*, Mr. Freeman, after referring to the doubtful authenticity of Edward the Confessor's charter, goes on: "doubtful as this charter is, the spuriousness of that which accompanies it (the charter of Robert Count of Mortain) is still more manifest." He then recites the fact that whereas the latter charter is dated 1085, it bears the signatures of Queen Matilda, who died in 1083, and of Bishop Leofric, who died in 1072; also the exemption from ecclesiastical jurisdiction granted by Leofric at the instance of Pope Gregory, who did not become Pope until after Leofric's death—altogether a most formidable indictment—and he proceeds to quote from the Exeter Domesday, with a view of establishing the real date of the foundation of St. Michael, the following passage (which will also be found below labelled A.):

"Sanctus Michahel habet i. mansionem quae vocatur Treiwal quam tenuit Brismarus eâ die qua Rex E. fuit vivus et mortuus. . . . De hac mansione abstulit Comes de Moritonio i. de praedictis ii. hidis quae erat de dominicatu beati Michahelis."

"This," he says, "is the only mention of the house I can find, and it would seem to imply a foundation between 1066 and 1085. Brismar was a man of large property in all the three shires. He is not unlikely to have been the founder of the Cornish Saint Michael, and if so he must have founded it, or at least have given the estate, after Edward's death."

[1] *Norman Conquest*, pp. 766, 767.

"It seems plain . . . that whoever was the founder of the Cornish house it was not Earl Robert." And he concludes, "a note in the *Monasticon* (vii. 989) speaks of another tradition as naming Robert's son William as the person who gave the Cornish house to the Norman one. Here we most likely have the clue to the mistake."

When therefore Mr. Round is found endorsing Mr. Freeman's opinion[1] that "Treiwal was given to St. Michael between the death of Edward the Confessor and the making of the great Survey," and suggesting that Earl Brian (who could have had no footing in England before the Conquest) may have been the founder, it may seem presumption to express an opinion clean contrary to both. But let Domesday Book tell its own story. There are three references in the Exeter Book and two in the Exchequer Book which bear upon the subject. They are given below and labelled A, B, C, D, E for convenience of reference—those portions only being omitted which do not concern the present discussion. The extensions are for the use of those who are not familiar with the abbreviated Latin text.

A. Exeter Domesday, fol. 208b. (Ed. 1816, p. 189).

Terra Sancti Michahelis de Cornugallia. Sanctus Michahel habet unam mansionem quae vocatur Treiwal quam tenuit Brismarus eâ die qua rex Edwardus fuit vivus et mortuus. In ea sunt ii hidae terrae quae nonquam reddiderunt gildam. Has possunt arare viii carrucae. Ibi habet Sanctus Michahel i carrucam. . . . De hac mansione abstulit comes de Moritonio i de praedictis ii hidis quae erat de dominicatu beati Michahelis.

[1] *Genealogist, N.S.*, XVII, 2.

B. *Ibid.*, fol. 508 (Ed. 1816, p. 471).

Sanctus Michael habet i mansionem quae vocatur Treiwal de qua abstulit comes de Moritonio i hidam, quae erat in dominicatu Sancti die qua rex Edwardus fuit vivus et mortuus.

C. *Ibid.*, fol. 258b (Ed. 1816, p. 138).

Comes habet i mansionem quae vocatur Treuthal quam tenuit Brismarus sacerdos eâ die qua rex Edwardus fuit vivus et mortuus. In ea est i hida terrae et reddit gildum·(sic) Sancto Michaele (sic). Hanc abstulit comes Sancto. Bluhidus Brito tenet eam de comite.

D. Exchequer Domesday, page ii, column 2.

Terra Sancti Michaelis. Ecclesia Sancti Michaelis tenet Treiwal. Brismar tenebat tempore Regis Edwardi. Ibi sunt ii hidae quae nunquam geldaverunt. . . . De his ii hidis abstulit comes Moritoniensis i hidam.

E. *Ibid.*, columns 1 and 2, 125 a and b.

Idem (Blohiu) tenet Trevthal. Brismar tenebat tempore Regis Edwardi . . . Hanc terram abstulit comes aecclesiae Sancti Michaelis.

The very title which introduces extract A is suggestive. The land of St. Michael " of Cornwall " implies another St. Michael just as " St. Ives in Cornwall " implies a St. Ives elsewhere. And it is this St. Michael of Cornwall and no other who " has one manor which is called Treiwal which Brismar held at the time of Edward the Confessor's death. There are two hides of land which have never paid geld. From this manor the Earl of Mortain has taken away one of the aforesaid two hides which was of Blessed Michael's demesne." If St. Michael of Cornwall did not exist before the Conquest it is difficult to understand how he could have had lands in demesne in the time of the Confessor. But it may be objected there is here no mention of the saint holding lands in the time of the Confessor. Accepting the correction for what it is worth, which is probably infinitesimal, because the whole tenor of the Domesday assessment—both as regards its ruling principle and its literary flavour—is found in the reiteration of the contrast or comparison of the land values as determined in the days of King Edward and at the time of the Survey, admitting the correction, let the reader refer to extract B. This reads, " St. Michael has one manor, which is called Treiwal, from which the Count of Mortain has taken away one hide which was in the demesne of the saint on the day upon which King Edward was alive and dead." St. Michael (of Cornwall) was, therefore, quite as truly alive at the decease of the Confessor as Edward was dead. In the light of what has been said consider extract C. This is important, because it tells us that Brismar was a priest and a very different person from the magnate described by Mr. Freeman who held lands in three shires.

Extract C also introduces us to Treuthal, which Brismar the priest held at the Confessor's death. " Therein is one hide and it renders geld to St. Michael." (The Domesday scribe, not the printer, is responsible for " gildum " and " Michaele.") " This the Count has taken away from the saint. Bluhid Brito (Blohiu of Brittany) holds it of the Count." No one who is acquainted with the history of Treuthal, with its almost endless variety of spellings, can doubt either where it was or what it was. It was the patrimony and the place of residence in the parish of Ludgvan of the Bloyou family, the descendants of Bluhid Brito (Ralph Bloyou was born there[1] on the Feast of the Nativity of the B.V.M. 21 Edward I) until 1354, when Elizabeth, daughter and heir of Alan Bloyou, sold it to Sir Nigel Loring.[2] It is still the name of a village and the name of a manor. While Treiwal, by which name the Domesday compiler seeks to distinguish St. Michael's land from Blohiu's, is almost, if not quite, forgotten, the variant Truthwall survives. But to revert to Brismar. Comparing A, B, and C, it is clear that one hide was taken away from Treiwal, that it was of Blessed Michael's demesne in the time of King Edward, that Brismar the priest held it in the time of King Edward, that the Count of Mortain took it away from St. Michael, that it, nevertheless, paid geld to St. Michael at the time of the Survey, that Blohiu held it of the Count at the time of the Survey, and that it was called Treuthal to distinguish it from Treiwal, the name of the parent manor. With these facts before us it is impossible to doubt that for fiscal purposes Brismar the priest and St. Michael the archangel were regarded as identical in the time of King Edward—in other words, Brismar was the visible representative of the invisible archangel. This explains why in extract D Brismar held Treuthal in the time of Edward, and why in extract E Brismar held, in Edward's time, that which "the Earl has taken away from the church of St. Michael."

[1] Chan. inq. p.m., 12 Edw. II, No 16.
[2] De Banco, 12 Henry VI, Hilary, m. 443.

There are two further considerations which may be adduced in support of the contention that St. Michael of Cornwall was the name of a religious community which was not, at the time of the Survey, identical with St. Michael of Normandy. It will strike every careful reader of that part of Domesday which relates to Cornwall that wherever a church or a saint is mentioned the reference is to what we now call either a conventual or a collegiate church.

St. Aliquis holds a manor which is called Quidvis, the church of St. Aliquis holds a manor which is called Quidvis—these are only different ways of saying that the manor of Quidvis belongs to the community of St. Aliquis. When, therefore, we read that one hide of Treiwal was of the demesne of St. Michael in the days of the Confessor, we know that the land belonged to a body of religious.

The second consideration is this: It has been pointed out to me that the phrase "nunquam geldaverunt" (have never paid geld) is also peculiar, in Cornwall, to quasi-monastic lands. But St. Michael not only did not pay geld, he received geld, and received it from that hide of land of which he had been despoiled by the Count.

Excluding St. German, who fared badly, the Count usurping all his demesne lands, and whose only dues had consisted of a cask of beer and 30d. paid to the church, there were ten such communities in Cornwall at the time of the Survey. Of these only three, St. Michael, St. Petrock and St. Stephen, ever became affiliated to the larger monastic bodies. The rest remained what they then were, collegiate churches, served by a body of secular canons, who in course of time disappeared, giving place to a rector. St.

Buryan was apparently the last of these communities to be dissolved. To sum up the results. It will, I think, be admitted that extract A is not the only mention of the house of St. Michael to be found in Domesday, that it was not founded between 1066 and 1085, that Brismar —the Brismar of St. Michael— was not a man of large property but a priest representing St. Michael, that if he founded the house it was before and not after the Conquest, and, finally, that for reasons already stated, Earl Brian was not the founder. Moreover, it is hardly likely that a body of ecclesiastics, either at Mont Michel or at St. Michael's Mount, would have cited Edward as the patron of the Cornish house if there had been some earlier patron to cite. It would rather seem that what Mr. Round says of Count Robert's charter is not far from the truth, viz. "the fact that the form of the charter as we have it is probably not genuine does not of necessity invalidate its substance."

In justice to Mr. Round it must be added that after reading the arguments here put forward, he would, in support of his contention, read the concluding words of extract B elliptically : "one hide which was in (what became) the saint's demesne on the day on which King Edward was alive or dead (i.e. after the Confessor's death)." It is clear that such a method of interpreting Domesday Book can only be allowable when there is overwhelming evidence in its favour. In this case the evidence does not seem to warrant its application.

As we have seen, Count Robert by his charter gives to the Norman house, St. Michael's Mount with half a hide of land and a market on Thursdays and lands in Amaneth. Comparing this statement with that of

Domesday Book, it will be observed that in the latter there is no mention of lands in Amaneth and no mention of the market, although in Domesday markets are frequently mentioned, while on the other hand there is mention made of two hides of land, one of which, Treuthal, the Count has taken from St. Michael to be held of him by Bloyou, the other being held by St. Michael in demesne. The question which arises is : Did the Count restore one half of the usurped lands or, assuming the charter to have been made before Domesday Book (1086) was compiled, did he by a later instrument add half a hide, thereby endowing St. Michael with a moiety of the hide held in demesne ? We know from the subsequent history of the lands under discussion that the Bloyous remained in possession of Truthall, which never had a market, and we know that a market was held at Marazion or thereabouts within the Domesday manor of Treiwal. We therefore conclude that the Count's gift to the Norman abbey was a further act of spoliation, which by connivance of the Conqueror he was allowed to practise against the Cornish monks, and also that his charter was executed subsequent to 1086. The presence of Queen Matilda's name among the witnesses is the only invalidating element in what we have every reason to regard as an authentic document. Its confirmation by Bishop Leofric, and also the bishop's postscript, are probably both of them forgeries. To give them the appearance of genuineness the Queen's name may have been added to the authentic document. Be that as it may, the alleged date, 1085, supposed to have been supplied by the bishop, is impossible, inasmuch as the fourteenth year of indiction with which it is made to synchronise would be either 1070 or 1094.

In 1094 the Conqueror was dead, and in 1070 "Henricus puer" was in the second year of his age. It must also be added that the date does not occur in the charter, but is supplied from the cartulary.

The composite character of the postscript to which also Leofric's signature is appended is seen in the wild statement to which it bears witness. In it we are informed that by command and counsel of Pope Gregory and of the King, Queen and Nobles of England, the bishop grants immunity from all episcopal control to the church of Blessed Michael the Archangel of Cornwall, and a remission of one-third of their penance to all who shall enrich, endow or visit it. Pope Gregory (Hildebrand) was not elected till 1073, the year after Leofric's death, and the indulgence which the postscript contains and which constitutes its *raison d'être* was manifestly only an expedient to foster pilgrimages to St. Michael's Mount which, supposing the monastery to have been founded after the Conquest, would have been too obvious to achieve its object. Something more will be said under this head when dealing with the testimony of William of Worcester.

When allowance has been made for clerical errors and for the interpolations and additions to which attention has been drawn, there is no sufficient reason to reject either the literal interpretation of Domesday or the authenticity of Edward's charter, or the substantial accuracy of Count Robert's. The date of the latter would probably be 1086, or a little later, probably in the last year of the Conqueror's reign. A third charter of the reign of William Rufus records the grant to the Norman St. Michael, by Count Robert of Mortain and Almodis his Countess of the manor of Ludgvan held by Richard Fitz Turold, also that which Bloyou formerly held in Truthwall (Treiuhalo), and both the fairs (*ferias*) of the Mount, the monks paying to the grantors the sum of sixty pounds.

Now it is worthy of remark that neither of these manors ever became permanently attached to either religious house. Though it is impossible to speak with certainty, it looks as if the Count had wrested Ludgvan from Richard, had claimed Truthwall on the death of Bloyou and had sold them both to the Norman abbot, who afterwards found it impossible to resist the claims of the rightful heirs.

The Cornish St. Michael had assuredly no cause to hold the Count in grateful remembrance. From first to last he acted the part of a robber. On this occasion one is inclined to suspect that the possessions of the brethren serving God at the Mount were much more extensive before than after the Norman Conquest. Assuming the Confessor's charter to be genuine it would almost appear that the Meneage district had, at a remote period, become attached to a Celtic monastery at the Mount, and that he was merely ratifying the title while perhaps limiting the extent of its possessions.

There is yet another document of great importance. It is described in the Otterton custumal[1] as the Erection (*Constructio*) of the Priory of St. Michael in Cornwall. It is, in reality, a notification by Bernard, abbot of the Norman house, that the church of Blessed Michael of Cornwall, built by him in 1135,

[1] Oliver, *Monasticon*, p. 414.

was consecrated in his presence by Robert (Chichester), bishop of Exeter, that, with the advice of the said Pontiff and of Count Raner, and with the approbation of the barons of the province, he has got together thirteen brethren and has made provision for them out of old endowments and current contributions, that he has enacted that he who shall be selected by the parent house to be prior of St. Michael's Mount shall not fail to make a return to it of 16 marks yearly, that if he shall prove refractory he shall be degraded and another prior appointed by the abbot with the abbey's consent, and so on. Moreover, the Cornish brethren are to receive the benediction of the monastic order from the abbot *in Monte Tumba* unless perchance it please him to come to Cornwall and bless them there. At the end of the instrument there is a list of the possessions of the Blessed Michael of Cornwall, given to the archangel by Count Robert of Mortain, viz. Tremaine, where there is sufficient land for two ploughs, Trahorabohc for three, Listyahavehet for three, Treganeis for two, Carmahelech for two.

The entire document is needlessly defiant and menacing. The Cornish house is reduced to a mere appanage of the abbey and the prior to a mere collector of 16 marks for its benefit. Every vestige of independence is swept away, and that, too, in subversion of the primary principle of the saintly founder of the order. One hardly expected to find evidence in Cornwall in confirmation of Dante's description given more than a century later.

> The walls, for abbey reared, turned into dens (of thieves),
> The cowls to sacks, choked up with musty meal.

It is therefore satisfactory to note that the priory

could only reckon among its possessions the lands given by the Count of Mortain, the rest of St. Michael's lands having either been confiscated or alienated between the date of the Domesday Survey (1086) and that of the document (1135).

To identify the several grants of land a more or less careful examination of the places mentioned in the charters becomes necessary. Taking them in order of date, the Confessor by his charter gives to St. Michael for the use of the brothers serving God the place known as St. Michael, which is by the sea, with all that belongs to it, and he adds the whole land of Vennefire, with its towns, vills and lands; also the port of Ruminella, with its mills and fisheries. One of the witnesses is Vinfred, or, as the name is commonly written, Winfred. We are therefore justified in substituting "W" for "V" in Vennefire, and "s" for "f" according to the Avranches cartulary. Vennefire becomes Wenneshire. A glance at the Feudal Aids reminds us that the hundreds of Cornwall were entered as Poudreschir (Powder), Pydrisire,[1] Pydar, Trigrishire, etc. It is therefore safe to regard Vennefire as the equivalent of Wenneshire. But the name of the hundred in Domesday Book is Wineton, a correlative, in this case the equivalent of Wenneshire. Vennefire is therefore the hundred of Kerrier. Ruminella is the diminutive or feminine, not only in Latin but in Welsh,[2] of Rumin or Rumon. The port of Ruminella thus becomes the port of Ruan Minor, i.e. Cadgwith. One or more mills still exist in the valley and at no great distance from the port. If, as we have already suggested, the

[1] Feudal Aids, 1303, 1306, etc.

[2] Loth, *Vie de Saint Samson*, p. 15.

Meneage district was, like the hundred of Pydar, settled by Celtic monks, the Confessor's grant would mean little more than the confirmation to them of their ancient patrimony, focussed at St. Michael's Mount.

Edward can hardly be supposed to have had an intimate knowledge of the locality or of its conditions. Under the influence of men like Robert of Jumièges he may well have given more than he had at his disposal. The futility of the attempt is the best proof of its having been made. It is certain that at the time of his death the monks of St. Michael had no considerable holding in Kerrier. Earl Harold had become overlord of the manor of Wineton, seventeen thegns holding eleven hides of him, the rest being held by him in demesne. After the Conquest Wineton fell to the King, who gave the whole to Robert Count of Mortain, to be held of the Count by sub-tenants. It may have been in some measure as an act of reparation, but it was chiefly in order to augment the influence and revenue of St. Michael of Normandy that he granted to that abbey St. Michael's Mount in Cornwall, with half a hide of land and three (Cornish) acres of land in Amaneth, to wit Trevelaboth, Lismanoch, Trequaners and Carmailoc. No conditions of tenure are specified except freedom from the King's jurisdiction in all matters but homicide. It is not stated, for example, whether the lands shall be held of the Cornish or of the Norman St. Michael. In some sense no doubt the community at the Mount became henceforth an alien priory of Mont St. Michel, but there does not seem to have been any definition of the relations between the two houses until 1135.

The identification of the names Amaneth, Trevelaboth, Lismanoch, Trequaners and Carmailoc is not free from difficulty. The word Amaneth is probably for An-maneth, i.e. An-manech, the monastic (territory) and equivalent to Meneage.[1] Manaccan the monk's (church) (cf. Plou-manach in Brittany, the monk's parish) is situated in the northern portion of what is still known as the Meneage district, which Leland (1533–1552) calls the land of Meneke or Menegland.

The next name—Trevelaboth—presents no difficulty. There is a continuous chain of evidence to show that it is identical with Traboe, a small manor in the parish of St. Keverne. In order to equate the three holdings which remain, viz. Lismanoch, Trequaners and Carmailoc, it will be necessary to refer to a document in the Otterton custumal[2] in which they appear as Tremain, Listyavehet, Treganeis and Carmaheleck. Carmailoc is obviously Carmaheleck or Carvallack, a holding in St. Martin's parish which derives its name from the prehistoric earthwork in that parish. If we suppose the "n" in Trequaners and Treganeis to be a false reading for "u"—a pardonable blunder of constant occurrence—we have the modern tenement of Tregevas or Tregevis also in St. Martin's. We are thus left with Lismanoch as the equivalent of Tremain (the modern Tremayne) and Listyavehet. Tremain calls for no remark in this connection: everyone knows where it is. Lismanoch,

[1] Anmaneth may be an Anglicised form of An-manegh (cf. Carnyorth and Respeth for Carnyorgh and Respegh), but it is more likely that Amaneth is an adjectival form, viz. Manéghek or Menaghek, which became successively Menéhek, Meneck, Menek, Meneage (cf. *infra* Trevanaek). I am indebted to Mr. Henry Jenner for this suggestion and for some other notes on the derivation of Cornish place-names.

[2] See appendix, p. 175.

of which it appears to have formed a portion, presents some difficulty, because in that form the name is now unknown. As Lesmanaoc it occurs in a grant of King Edgar in 967 to Wulfnod Rumancant. In that grant its boundaries are minutely described, but unfortunately to little purpose owing to the fact that many of the place-names in it are either purely descriptive or have become so altered during the ten centuries which have elapsed since the grant was made as to be incapable of recognition. One or two points are clear. Lesmanaoc was of considerable extent. For some distance it lay along the river which empties itself at Porthallow. It must have reached well towards the south of St. Keverne parish if "Castell Merit" and "Crouswrah" (two places mentioned in the charter) are, as seems probable, the modern tenement of Kestlemerris and Crousa Downs. At the time of Count Robert's charter its area had evidently been contracted, otherwise it could hardly have escaped mention in Domesday Book. The portion which had been lost was probably the southern portion, for no mention is made of any possessions south of Traboe in the grants of the priory lands after its dissolution.

These considerations lend support to what is something more than a conjecture of Mr. Henry Jenner, viz. that in the two tenements now known as Lesneage we have the site of Lesmanaoc. Lesneage, as he points out, may well be a contracted form of Lesmeneage, which in turn may be only another form of Lesmanaoc, on the same principle as Treveneage in St. Hilary can be shown by an unbroken series of documents to have been derived from Trevanaek.

It is worthy of remark that within a short distance

of Lesneage is Mill Mehal or St. Michael's Mill. If this be the true etymology then the name Listyavehet becomes less formidable than it looks.

The final "t" is the only difficulty. If we may regard it as a false reading for "l," Listyavehet becomes Lis-ty-amehel, the "court of the house of St. Michael," Lesmanaoc being the "Monk's Court," and the change of name easily accounted for by the transfer of the monks' possessions in Menegland (monastic land) to the house at St. Michael's Mount.

The *Itinerary* of William of Worcester deserves attention. It is a curious assortment of undigested and ill-arranged odds and ends of information compiled in the year 1478, that is to say about half a century after the expulsion of the Benedictines from the Mount and the introduction of the Bridgettines, only five years after the Mount was seized by John de Vere, Earl of Oxford, and surrendered by him to the King's troops after a siege of twenty-three weeks. The *Itinerary* is properly speaking a note-book. For the most part William confines himself to matters of topography, genealogy and hagiology.

Once and again he condescends to men of low estate, as, for example, when he tells us that about the year 1476 one Thomas Clerk, of Ware, left Ware on the Octave of St. John the Baptist and rode to the Mount within ten days and then returned to Ware at the end of another ten days, thereby covering, according to the route bill which is given, something over thirty-two miles a day for twenty consecutive days. William himself rode more leisurely. Leaving Norwich on the 16th of August, 1478, travelling by way of Truro, he reached Marazion on the 16th of September. The next day he heard Mass at the Mount and in the afternoon of the same day he began the return journey to Penryn. The time spent by him in Cornwall was just over a week.

That he should have gathered as much material as he did is therefore a matter for surprise. Towards this harvest St. Michael's Mount contributed its full share, which is scattered without any regard for convenience or context throughout the work. After describing the tributaries of the river Fal, and à propos of nothing whatever, he inserts a (supposed) indulgence of Pope Gregory, said to have been granted by him in 1070, although Hildebrand did not become Pope until three years later. The indulgence is addressed to the church of Mount St. Michael in Tumba in the County of Cornwall, and of it, all but the opening words are a verbatim copy of the spurious postscript to the Count of Mortain's charter, of which mention has been already made. It is followed by a notice added by the Community at the Mount stating that the document, having been recently discovered in the old registers, is placed on the church door and, being unknown to most men, they, the ministers and servants of God, require and beg all who have the guidance of souls to do all in their power to publish it in their churches so that their subjects may be moved to greater devotion and may, by pilgrimage, frequent that place and obtain the said gifts and indulgences. William next mentions the apparition of St. Michael in Mount Tumba, formerly called the "Hore-rok in the Wodd," which happened at a time when woodland and meadow and plough land lay between the said Mount and the islands of Scilly, and there were 240 parish churches now submerged.

He observes that the first apparition of St. Michael in Mount Gorgon in the Kingdom of Apulia took place in A.D. 391 ; the second, in Tumba in Cornwall, near the sea, about A.D. 710 ; the third, in the days of Pope Gregory at a time of a great pestilence ; the fourth being *in ierarchiis nostrorum angelorum.* The next paragraph appears to be the fragment of a description of Mont St. Michel and its foundation by St. Aubert, bishop of Avranches.

Then follow various measurements. The length of the church of Mount St. Michael is stated to be 30 "steppys," its breadth 12 steppys ; the length of the chapel newly built is 40 feet, i.e. 20 steppys ; its breadth about 10 steppys ; from the church to the foot of the Mount, to the sea-water, 14 times 60 steppys ; the distance by sea between Marazion and the foot of the Mount is estimated at 1200 (feet), i.e. 700 steppys, in English 10 times 70 steppys. It is difficult to reconcile the last of these measurements with the former and to connect the "step" with a modern equivalent. The "step" was not a "pace," for speaking of the dimensions of Bodmin Church, William says in length it is 57 paces (*passus*) and in breadth 30 steppys. It was apparently two feet (*pedes*), but whether two modern feet of 12 inches we are unable to say. A little further on William tells us that the island of St. Michael's Mount is about a mile in diameter and is distant from the mainland the length of a bow-shot. It lies north of the island of Ushant in Brittany.

After dealing with the Bodmin martyrology, information given by Robert Bracey at Fowey and the kalendar of Tavistock, he mentions the capture and surrender of the Mount by the Earl of Oxford five years before the time of his writing. A fuller notice occurs towards the end of his work where, after some further details respecting the Mount's geographical position, he gives us the kalendar of the church. The saints commemorated are, as has been already remarked, with three exceptions all Celtic. Of one of them, Brokan (Brychan) and his twenty-four children, he supplies an account taken, as it would seem, from the Legenda. For in the enumeration the saint is described as Brokannus in partibus Walliarum *regulus fide et morum*, and in the account of the saint which follows the opening sentence is Fuit in ultinus (ultimis) Walliarum partibus vir dignitate *regulus fide et morum* honestate praeclarus, nomine Brokannus. A similar explanation may account for the fourth apparition of St. Michael being described by William as apparicio in ierarchiis nostrorum angelorum, a phrase which is meaningless as it stands, but assuming it to be a quotation from the Legenda may have been familiar and intelligible to William's readers.

From the foregoing abstracts from the *Itinerary* two conclusions appear to be inevitable. In the first place, whether of design or by inadvertence, the name Mons Tumba which had been exclusively used of the Norman Mount came to be also applied to the Cornish Mount and, in the second place, the associations of the former came to be adopted by the latter. The postscript to the Count of Mortain's charter and the newly discovered indulgence mentioned by William, the one an almost verbatim copy of the other, probably bear witness to a fact, namely, that an indulgence was actually granted by Pope Gregory, but that it was granted not to St. Michael's Mount but to Mont St. Michel. When once the indulgence had been appropriated by the Cornish house it became necessary to account for the allusions contained in it. The ecclesia quae ministerio angelico creditur et comprobatur consecrari et sanctificari demanded some point d'appui, and this could only be obtained by increasing the number of apparitions vouchsafed by St. Michael.

The three apparitions generally accepted by Western Christendom, viz. the appearance in the fifth century to Garganus, that in the sixth century to St. Gregory at Rome, and that in the eighth century (A.D. 706) to St. Aubert, bishop of Avranches (probably identical with the apparicio in ierarchiis nostrorum angelorum), were supplemented by an appearance (A.D. 710) in Tumba in Cornwall. It is impossible to say when this claim was formulated, whether before or after the expulsion of the Benedictines in the fifteenth century. The object was evidently to stimulate pilgrimages, concerning which, however, very little is recorded. Norden, writing in 1584, states that the Mount "hath bene muche resorted unto by Pylgrims in devotion to St. Michaell whose chayre is fabled to be in the Mount, on the south syde, of verie Daungerous access."

When William of Worcester visited the Mount the priory was in possession of Augustinian nuns known as Bridgettines. Of them William says nothing.

So long as it was Benedictine and under the control of the abbot of Mont St. Michel, successive Kings of England felt constrained, on the declaration of war with France, to take it into their own hands and to administer its preferment. From 1337 onwards the rolls contain numerous entries dealing with the patronage of alien priories. During his war with

France Henry IV required the prior of St. Michael's Mount to hold the priory at farm for a yearly rent of £10. Henry V, having founded the abbey of Syon in Middlesex, transferred the priory to it, the provost and scholars of the college of St. Mary and St. Nicholas at Cambridge, to whom an earlier grant of it seems to have been made, surrendering all their rights in 1462.

Thenceforth until 1536 it remained a Bridgettine nunnery. After the suppression of the monasteries several grants were made of it for terms of years. Eventually Queen Elizabeth sold it to Robert, Earl of Salisbury, by whose son, the second earl, it was conveyed to Sir Francis Basset. By his son, John Basset, it was sold in 1659 to Colonel St. Aubyn. Since that time it has remained in the St. Aubyn family, its present owner and occupier being General John Townshend St. Aubyn, second Lord St. Levan.

With its religious history alone are we here concerned. That the Mount was the home of a Celtic religious community in pre-Norman times hardly admits of doubt. As we have shown, there was some strong bond of attachment between it and the Meneage, a bond which, though weakened and attenuated, was not completely sundered until the dissolution of the monasteries in the sixteenth century. The main proposition here advanced is that the Mount was at a remote period, probably as early as the days of St. Cadoc, the focus of Celtic religious activity for the greater part, if not for the whole, of the Lizard peninsula.

APPENDIX A

Extract from the "Life of St. Samson"
(Ed. by Fawtier, pp. 143–5)

QUADAM autem die, cum per quendam pagum quem Tricurium vocant deambularet, audivit, ut verum esset, in sinistra parte de eo, homines baccantum ritu quoddam· phanum per imaginariam ludum adorantes; atque ille annuens fratribus ut starent et silerent dumque quiete, et ipse de curru ad terram descendens et ad pedes stans, intendensque in his qui idolum colebant, vidit ante eos in cujusdam vertice montis, simulacrum abominabile adsistere; in quo monte et ego fui, signumque crucis quod sanctus Samson sua manu cum quodam ferro in lapide stante sculpsit adoravi et mea manu palpavi; quod sanctus Samson, ut vidit, festine ad eos, duos apud se tantum fratres eligens, properavit atque ne idolum, unum Deum qui creavit omnia, relinquentes, colere deberent, suaviter commonuit, adstante ante eos eorum comite Guediano; atque excusantibus illis malun non esse mathematicum eorum parentum in ludo servare, aliis furentibus, aliis deridentibus, non nullis autem quibus mens erat sanior ut abiret hortantibus, continuo adest virtus Dei publice ostensa. Nam puer quidam equos in cursu dirigens a quodam veloci equo ad terram cecidit collumque ejus subtus se praecipitem plicans, exanimum paene corpus in jecturam tantum remansit.

Flentibus autem circa illum vicinis suis, sanctus Samson dixit "Videtis quod simulacrum vestrum non potest huic mortuo adjutorium dare? Si autem promittitis vos hoc idolum penitus destruere et non amplius adorare ego illum, Deo in me operante, redivivum resuscitabo." Adquiescentibus autem illis, jussit eos paulo longius secedere, atque illo orante super exanimem per binas ferme horas, illum qui expiratus fuerat redivivum palam omnibus atque incolumem redidit. Videntibus autem illis, unanimes omnes una cum supradicto comite, procidentes ad sancti Samsonis pedes, idolum penitus destruxerunt.

The Reverend F. W. Paul, M.A., whose friendship it has been my privilege to share for half a century, has revised the translation on page 33. He has done so under protest. Incompetence, ignorance of monkish Latin and the corruptness of the text have been his pleas. The first no one will allow who knows him ; the second is by no means uncommon ; the third everyone will admit. L'Abbé Duine truly says of the *Vita Samsonis* that *plusieurs constructions grammaticales sont absolument barbares.* Mr. Paul has suggested the following emendations of the passage before us. Although drastic they appear worthy of consideration, unless they can be shown to run clean contrary to the habits of thought, the terminology and the rules of composition observed by writers of the seventh century. For quoddam phanum he would read *quendam phallum ;* for mathematicum, *matrimonium ;* for injecturam, *jecturâ.* We should then have in the latter part of the first sentence "he saw men worshipping a certain phallus after the custom of the Bacchantes by means of a lewd play," and for *atque excusantibus illis malum non esse mathematicum eorum parentum in ludo servare,* "and when they said that there was no harm in their commemorating their parents' wedlock in a play." I have accepted *jecturâ* for in jecturam and his translation of it. It is unfortunate that a critical edition of the *Vita Samsonis* has not yet been prepared. L'Abbé Duine has indeed furnished some useful notes—only too few—on the syntax and the peculiar use of certain pronouns, prepositions and adjectives.[1] But, as Professor Loth truly observes, to produce such an edition a minute study of the syntax is required and also a glossary of all the words which in form or in meaning are peculiar—a glossary in which all the idioms should be exhibited. The task requires special qualifications and will not perhaps appeal strongly to those who have them. Sooner or later someone will doubtless be found to undertake it, someone, it is hoped, who is not only a scholar but who is familiar with the religious literature of the seventh and eighth centuries.

[1] Duine, *Saints de Domnonée*, pp. 5–12.

APPENDIX B

Edward the Confessor's Charter
(Oliver's *Monasticon*, p. 31)

Carta Edwardi regis Anglorum pro abbatiâ sancti Michaelis (Ex autographo apud S. Michaelem in Normannia).

IN nomiñe sanctae et individuae Trinitatis, ego Edwardus Dei gratia Anglorum rex, dare volens pretium redemptionis animae meae, vel parentum meorum, sub consensu et testimonio bonorum virorum, tradidi sancto Michaeli archangelo in usum fratrum Deo servientium in eodem loco sanctum Michaelem qui est juxta mare, cum omnibus appendenciis, villis scilicet, castellis, agris et caeteris attinentibus. Addidi etiam totam terram de Vennefire,[1] cum oppidis, villis, agris, pratis, terris cultis et incultis, et cum horum redditibus. Adjunxi quoque datis portum addere qui vocatur Ruminella cum omnibus quae ad eum pertinent, hoc est molendinis et piscatoriis et cum omni territorio illius culto et inculto, et eorum redditibus.

Si quis autem his donis conatus fuerit ponere calumpniam anathema factus, iram Dei incurrat perpetuam. Utque nostrae donationis auctoritas verius firmiusque teneatur in posterum, manu meâ firmando subterscripsi, quod et plures fecere testium.

Signum regis Edwardi ✠ Signum Roberti archiepiscopi Rothomagensis ✠ Hereberti episcopi Lexoviensis. Roberti episcopi Constantiensis. Signum Radulphi ✠ Signum Vinfredi ✠ Nigelli vicecomitis. Anschitilli. Choschet. Turstini.

[1] "Vennesire" in the cartulary at Avranches.

APPENDIX C

Charter of Count Robert of Mortain
(*Monasticon*, p. 31)

Carta Roberti, Comitis, pro monachis S. Michaelis.

IN nomine sanctae et individuae Trinitatis, Patris et Filii et Spiritus Sancti, amen. Ego Robertus Dei gratiâ Moritonii comes, igne divini amoris succensus, notifico omnibus sanctae ecclesiae matris nostrae filiis, habens in bello sancti Michaelis vexillum, quoniam pro animae meae salute atque meae conjugis, seu pro salute, prosperitate, incolumitate Gulielmi gloriosissimi regis, atque pro adipiscendo vitae aeternae premio, do et concedo Montem Sancti Michaelis de Cornubia Deo et monachis ecclesiae Sancti Michaelis de Periculo Maris servientibus, cum dimidiâ terrae hidâ, ita solutam et quietam ac liberam, ut ego tenebam, ab omnibus consuetudinibus querelis et placitis ; et constituo etiam ut ipsi monachi, concedente domino meo rege, ibidem mercatum die quintae feriae habeant. Postea autem, ut certissimè comperi beati Michaelis meritis monachorumque suffragiis michi a Deo ex propriâ conjuge meâ filio concesso, auxi donum ipsi beato militiae celestis Principi, dedi et dono in Amaneth tres acras terrae, Trevelaboth videlicet, Lismanoch, Trequaners, Carmailoc, annuente piissimo domino meo Gulielmo rege cum Mathilde reginâ atque nobilibus illorum filiis Roberto comite, Gulielmo Rufo, Henrico adhuc puero, ita quietam ae liberam de omnibus placitis querelis atque forisfactis, ut de nullâ re regiae justitiae monachi respondebunt nisi de solo homicidio. Hanc autem donationem feci ego

Robertus comes Moritonii, quam concesserunt gloriosus rex Anglorum Willielmus atque regina et filii eorum, sub testimonio istorum.

Signum Willielmi regis ✠. Signum reginae Mathildis ✠. Roberti comitis ✠. Willielmi Rufi filii regis ✠. Henrici pueri ✠. Roberti comitis Moritonii ✠. Matildis Comitissae ✠. Willielmi filii eorum ✠. Signum Willielmi filii Osberni ✠. Signum Rogeri de Monte - gomeri ✠. Tossetini vicecomitis ✠. Guarini ✠. Turulfi ✠.

Firmata abque roborata est hec carta, anno millessimo octuagesimo quinto ab incarnatione Domini indictione decimâ quartâ, concurrente tertiâ, lunâ octavâ, apud Pevenesel.

Signum Liurici Essecestriae Episcopi ✠.

Ego quidem Liuricus Dei dono Essecestriae episcopus, jussione et exhortatione domini mei reverentissimi Gregorii (VI) papae regisque nostri et reginae omniumque optimatum totius regni Angliae exhortatus ut ecclesiam beati Michaelis archangeli de Cornubia, utpote quae officio et ministerio angelico creditur atque comprobatur consecrari ac sanctificari, quatenus eam ab omni episcopali jure, potestate, seu subjectione liberarem atque exuerem, quod et facere totius cleri nostri consensu et hortatu non distuli, libero igitur eam et exuo ab omni episcopali dominatione, subjectione, inquietudine, et omnibus illis qui illam ecclesiam suis cum beneficiis et elemosinis expetierint, et visitaverint, tertiam partem penitentiarum condonamus. Et ut hoc inconcussum et immobile et etiam inviolabile fine tenus permaneat, ex authoritate Patris et Filii et Spiritus Sancti omnibus nostris successoribus interdicimus ne aliquid contra hoc decretum usurpare praesumant.

Signum ejusdem Liurici Essecestriae episcopi ✠.

APPENDIX D

Erection of the Priory of St. Michael in Cornwall
(*Monasticon*, p. 414)

Prioratûs St. Michaelis in Cornubiâ constructio (Ex custumali Prioratûs de Otterton, fol. 58).

OMNIBUS Sancte Dei ecclesie filiis notificare dignum duximus quod ecclesia beati Michaelis de Cornubia a venerabili Bernardo, ecclesie prefati archangeli de Periculo Maris abbate, in anno quo hominem exuit rex Henricus constructa, et in anno regis Stephani a religioso viro Roberto Exoniensi presule prestito abbate, qui presens aderat, id impetrante, Domino est consecrata. Idem vero abbas sagaci mente pertractans celestis militie principem locum eundem Deo ad serviendum et sibi ad inhabitandum delegisse, predicti pontificis consilio et comitis Raneri et baronum provincie suffragio, ut divinitati honor perpetuus impenderetur, officinas religioni idoneas construere et fratres xiii in honorem Christi Jhesu et apostolorum ejus, ut, videlicet, pro modulo suo in fide que per dilectionem operatur et spe in cultura vinee Domini Sabbaoth desudantis denarium mereretur retributionis, aggregare curavit ; de redditibus ecclesie tam antiquitus datis quam a viris provincie in presentia sua ad hoc attributis victui eorum necessario sufficienter providens.

Constituit autem ut vel per se vel per alium e fratribus ecclesiam de Monte in Normannia qui ex abbatis loci ejusdem precepto prioris in Cornubia fungetur officio annis singulis invisere non negligat, et argenti marchas xvi finetenus reddat. Quod si constitutioni huic obviare, vel contra abbatem suum vel conventum in aliquo presumpserit contraire, de prioratu suo degradetur, et alius pro abbatis arbitrio et conventus abbatie consilio subrogetur. Si vero superbus fuerit et contumax et prelatis ecclesie de Monte in Normannia inobediens extiterit, omni participatione totius beneficii ecclesie totius dicte, omniumque ecclesiarum ipsi societate aliqua connexarum, excommunicationi se deleat. Frates quidem, qui in Cornubia sancte conversationis habitum susceperint, monochatus jura in Monte Tumba profitentes, benedictionem monastici ordinis ab abbate suo ibidem suscepturos se noverint, nisi forte ei in Cornubiam venienti eos illuc benedicere placuerit. Hoc itaque tam justa Dei dispensatione tamque virorum sapientum discretione patratum, quicunque sive princeps sive potestas aliquam infringere presumpserit, videlicet, monachorum numerum qui pro facultatum ampliatione, et ipse ampliandus est, imminuat, et jam dicti loci possessiones in usus alteros convertat, ipsum, in quantum nobis a Domino collata est potestas, anathematis innodamus vinculo et hujus retributionem sceleris a justo judice suscipiat in futuro. Quicunque autem possessiones easdem conservare et pro suarum modulo facultatum, quia valuit Zachee rerum suarum multa distributio, valuerunt etiam vidue minuta duo, et regnum Dei tantum valet quantum homines, augmentare curaverunt, omnium se orationum totiusque beneficii ecclesie beate Michaelis de Monte in Normannia participes esse sciant.

He sunt possessiones quas ex dono comitis Roberti de Mortenio ecclesia beati Michaelis de Cornubia tenet: Tremaine, ubi ad duas carucas terra sufficiens habetur: Trahorabohc, ubi ad tres; Listyavehet, ubi ad tres; Treganeis, ubi ad duas; Carmahelech, ubi ad duas. Adjacet terra preter pascua ad omnia animalia necessaria; que simul caruce xii faciunt.

GENERAL INDEX

WILLIAM BRENDON AND SON, LTD., PLYMOUTH, ENGLAND